THE TALENT MANDATE

ALSO BY THE AUTHOR

Good for Business: The Rise of the Conscious Corporation (2009)

Consumed: Rethinking Business in the Era of Mindful Spending (2010)

THE TALENT MANDATE

WHY SMART COMPANIES PUT PEOPLE FIRST

ANDREW BENETT
WITH W. BARKSDALE MAYNARD AND ANN O'REILLY

palgrave
macmillan

CONTENTS

FOREWORD

A COUPLE OF YEARS AGO, ANDREW AND I WERE ENJOYING
one of our occasional get-togethers, comparing notes on work,
life, the universe, and points in between. I was deep into the
process of trying to turn a respected but troubled traditional magazine
business into a twenty-first-century media brand. The media industry
was frantically talking about its own impending doom, casting itself as
the poster child of a business model disrupted by digital technology and
changing consumer habits. My colleagues at *The Atlantic* and I faced what
felt like a life-or-death situation—How do you reverse decades of losses in
the midst of an economic and industry crisis? When I tallied up where and
how I was spending my time, I realized I was investing the vast majority
of my waking hours on issues related to talent: attracting and recruiting
talent; coaching, mentoring, and retaining talent; and figuring out how
to leverage our talent more successfully. I can now say with certainty that
talent was the crucial factor for *The Atlantic*'s ultimate turnaround and
survival, head and shoulders more important than any other contributing
factor. This idea resonated with Andrew; it turned out that he had been
having his own talent epiphanies in the context of the advertising industry
and crystallizing them in speeches and articles.

The more we talked, the more we found that we were thinking along
similar lines. Our business issues were different, but for both of us talent
was the factor that trumped everything else: It was the superingredient

that counted far more than any other. Talent was the problem and talent was the solution, but was that just for us, in our businesses? It had certainly come up a lot in conversations with our respective peers and clients, but maybe we were getting carried away. Maybe it was just the enthusiasm of old friends enjoying dinner and drinks and finding common ground. Was talent really such a big deal for leaders in other businesses in the cold light of day?

Andrew decided to find out. As you will discover, he has confirmed beyond doubt that talent is not just the focus of the HR and recruiting department; it is a burning issue for leaders across a whole range of organizations, from seat-of-the-pants startups to long-established multinationals to federal agencies and nonprofits. The range of organizations covered in this book says a lot about both Andrew's broad perspective on the issue and the importance of talent in the twenty-first century.

In the time since that get-together, my thinking about talent has evolved. If anything, I think we may have underestimated just how important a factor it has been in our business experiences. I knew from the start of my tenure that reviving the fortunes of a loss-making media brand in a disrupted industry was going to take a lot more than some smart leadership from the top. We needed to inject into our business the sort of adaptive, flexible, and creative talent that could create, build, and transform rather than maintain the declining status quo. Despite being more than 150 years old, we needed to think and act like a brand-new venture capital–funded startup. In every position, including creative editorial roles, we needed entrepreneurs keen to reinvent the business and find new ways of creating value with our venerable brand.

Talent with proven success in the digital space—digital natives—became priority hires. They had a resounding impact and set new standards, making them the core of our reinvented culture. However, adaptable digital immigrants also were vital to our process of renewal; they helped maintain the sense of history and brand quality standards that allowed us to stand out in increasingly commoditized online media and journalism. Their standards helped attract the quality digital native talent that we needed to be distinctive and true to our brand in the emerging media environment.

Finding this talent was nearly impossible. But as our business depended on it, we made it an organizational principle: We invented programs and processes for finding needles in haystacks. For example, every June, America's largest multibillion-dollar businesses go recruiting on campus at America's top 20 universities, and our little Atlantic Media Group was there too, one of the only media companies in the midst of big-name consulting firms and investment banks. The annual Atlantic Media Fellowship program is another initiative we developed to tap talent, reaching out to all the top graduating and recently graduated talent seeking careers in the journalism and media field. We devised national talent contests that culminated in recruiting weekends where our top executives acted as panels of judges across a series of programmed events: a cocktail party, a one-hour writing assignment, murder boards, team exercises, and talks with some of our top journalists—all part of a carefully constructed process to whittle thousands of candidates down to a chosen few.

Our obsession with talent paid off in more ways than "just" our survival, profitability, and growth—although those were certainly welcome fruits of our efforts. It was particularly gratifying when the judges at the 2013 Digiday Publishing Awards called us "a digital powerhouse" and nominated Atlantic Media as Publisher of the Year alongside two of America's hottest digital media startups, Vox Media and BuzzFeed. There's an important message in that distinction for readers of this book and for businesses everywhere: By putting talent front and center, even a failing 150-year-old company in a declining industry can reinvent itself and stand alongside thrusting newcomers. Reading through the many insights of this book, you will find plenty of reasons to make talent your core competency.

—Justin B. Smith,
CEO,
Bloomberg Media Group

PREFACE

STARTING A
CONVERSATION ON TALENT

YOU MAY BE ASKING YOURSELF WHY AN EXECUTIVE from the world of marketing communications, an industry not exactly renowned for doing a top-flight job with talent, has chosen to write a book about it. The short answer is that I am deeply passionate about talent—and determined to get it right—because I work in a field that creates success not through its products but through its people. And in the 20 years I have been in marketing, I have seen firsthand that talent is the single most important factor in guaranteeing a business's success.

As global president of Havas Worldwide, I work with 11,000 employees spread out over 316 offices in 120 cities and 75 countries. We provide advertising, marketing, corporate communications, and digital and social media solutions to a diverse array of world-class clients, including Air France, BNP Paribas, Citigroup, Danone Group, IBM, Lacoste, Merck, Mondelēz International, Pernod Ricard, Reckitt Benckiser, Sanofi, and other leading brands.

As I fly around the globe to meet with clients at these companies and others, I find executives all talking about the astonishing pace of change that has gripped their various industries. Everywhere you look, things have been transformed since 2000—and nowhere more so than in the role that talent management can play in creating value. Despite all the dialogue around the handling of talent, however, it is a competency that most organizations, large and small, have yet to develop fully. Far too often, talent management remains hobbled by outmoded ways of thinking.

Yet it has never been more critical. Companies are scrambling to become more nimble, increasingly valuing T-shaped employees who combine vertical expertise with the experience and ability to work across functions. As everything has gotten more competitive, organizations have had no choice but to be in the market and on their game every day to capture and retain the very best people.

Amid all the chaos and confusion, one lesson stands out to me: Having the right talent—and creating an environment in which they will flourish—is now the prime differentiator between companies that innovate and grow and those that are doomed to stagnate and sputter out.

There have been many books written about talent over the years, bulging with the accumulated wisdom of corporate management gurus, and yet there has been little real advancement on the ground. The soundest management theories have never been adequately reflected in workplace practices. One business school professor told me that no business function today lags behind so dramatically as talent; he sees improvements and innovations in every area except in the vital matter of managing people.

Frankly, that is discouraging to me, and not just because I care ardently about the issue. There is a cold, hard calculation at work here too: Because people costs tend to be upward of 50 percent of many industries' expense bases, nothing could be more vital than talent to the bottom line.

This book is my attempt to change the conversation about talent. I want to make it the C-suite and boardroom priority it deserves to be. In the pages that follow, I will share insights gleaned from my work running companies in which our success (and failure) hinged on our people. I have also had the pleasure of learning from hundreds of leaders who have cracked the talent code. What these people know—and what I aim to prove to you—is that talent will be the single most critical differentiating factor in business success in the tumultuous years that lie ahead.

If you do not grab the very best talent and nurture and grow them, rest assured your competitors will swipe them—and your business opportunities—right out from under you. Survival lies one way; extinction, the other. And talent makes all the difference.

PART I

THE TRANSFORMED BUSINESS ENVIRONMENT

CHAPTER 1

THE BIG SHIFT

Access to talented and creative people is to modern business what access to coal and iron ore was to steel-making.
—*Richard Florida, trends expert*

THE WORLD OF BUSINESS HAS ALWAYS HAD A FEARSOME reputation for being complicated, cutthroat, and unforgiving in its speed. But today the pressure is greater than ever, as unprecedented levels of competition and the breakneck pace of change mean companies must adapt on the run or risk falling irrevocably behind. This applies to virtually every aspect of the game, from infrastructure to finances, but most especially to talent management.

Think how much has changed in less than a century: Employee management has evolved from individual owners directly hiring, training, and managing workers to the massive, sometimes bloated undertaking we have come to know as human resource management. I don't know anyone who is particularly fond of the term *human resources* (*HR*), itself a 1970s replacement of *personnel*; for that matter, I don't know anyone who looks in the mirror and actually sees a human resource peering back. There is something vaguely Orwellian about the whole concept.

Regardless of the terminology used, what we have now in midsize and larger companies are multiple layers of professionals charged with the functions that business owners used to perform on their own—hiring, training, and firing—while also being tasked with myriad modern responsibilities such as managing benefits packages, promoting wellness goals, and monitoring employees' digital behavior. This new system has succeeded in taking a huge weight off the boss, but all too often it has come at the expense of distancing the chief executive and C-suite from the vital front lines of talent management. That is a big problem. And it is a problem that can only be solved with a major shift in focus on the part of top executives.

A CHANGED LANDSCAPE

To understand how the talent situation has gotten so far out of whack, we must first recognize the macro shifts that have changed the talent equation over the past century. These are:

- The shift from workers to talent
- The rise of the ideas economy
- The end of "jobs for life" and the beginning of Brand You

THE SHIFT FROM WORKERS TO TALENT

Cordoning off personnel management within a specialized department may not have posed such huge risks in the era preceding today's information economy. Back then, successful companies merely needed to find more and more "workers"—bodies to fill the slots and take care of whatever functions could not be automated fully. But it is an entirely different story now that most businesses fundamentally rely not on workers but on talent.

That is more than a semantic difference. Workers, it seems to me, bring to the job little more than functional competencies, whether it is loading boxes or filling out accounting records. Workers perform tasks almost mechanically according to instructions they have been given—typically doing things "the way they have always been done." The truly

talented, by contrast, make things happen by their fiery individual aptitudes, ideas, and drive. They add something to the equation that is unique
and nonreplicable. In today's transformed business world, the right combination of talent—managed and motivated in just the right way—is critical to creating the sort of differentiating value that supports long-term
success. Enterprises simply cannot thrive without it.

Not convinced? Consider the impact just one talented person can
have: How different would Apple be today if it hadn't hired Jonathan
Ive, the young British designer who went on to design the iPod? How
might the product lines of struggling Dell be different had Ive gone there
instead?

The job of identifying, soliciting, and managing talent is so crucial
now, it simply must not be left to an unprepared and unenthusiastic cadre
of managers or those schooled solely in the HR discipline. Setting the
agenda for the care and handling of talent can only properly be handled
by one person: the chief executive officer.

THE RISE OF THE IDEAS ECONOMY

In the Industrial Age, products were king. Henry Ford built an empire
based on mass-producing automobiles via assembly lines. Andrew Carnegie
forged his fortune with iron and steel. Today, business success is more likely
to center on something far less tangible: ideas. Knowledge, information,
and creative innovation are the new building blocks of wealth and success.
Billions have flowed to companies that have crafted cutting-edge information technologies (Intel, Microsoft, Cisco, Google) or applied computer-
aided design and manufacturing to make older processes more efficient
and profitable (DreamWorks, BMW).

What does this mean for talent management? It means that success
is no longer about fine-tuning production processes to churn out more
products with the same number of workers; instead, it is about fine-
tuning the employee base to produce knockout ideas and build a level of
value that vastly exceeds what each individual costs the company in pay
and benefits.

Plenty of bright people have the education, training, and skill sets that today's employers need, but those basics are no longer enough. In the old-fashioned, mechanical-industrial world, an employee's performance depended on easily quantifiable variables such as experience and training. The requirements of any job were clear in advance, and the right employees were those who slotted right in and got on with doing the job competently. But fewer and fewer organizations do this simplistic kind of work anymore. Now high-level skills have to be combined with more rarified aptitudes. What most of us are looking for—or should be looking for—are employees who do not simply fill a position but create one unique to them.

> What most of us are looking for—or should be looking for—are employees who do not simply fill a position but create one unique to them.

At a time when five-year plans are instantly obsolete, when companies audaciously expand into not just new product areas but entirely unexpected categories, when competitors emerge seemingly out of nowhere, the right employees are the ones who can grasp the big picture, anticipate what is coming next, constantly learn new skills—indeed, who can shape-shift at will. These people are out there—I know; I have hired a bunch of them—but they are an elusive group that can be hard to spot, harder to snare, and hardest of all to retain.

How did the talent equation get so complicated? Some credit must go to the twentieth century's fundamental overhaul of the employer-employee compact.

FROM COMPANY MAN TO BRAND YOU

Remember "jobs for life"? They're gone.

Intensified global competition, economic downturns, automation, and many other disruptive forces have combined to make lifelong employment all but obsolete. Companies have had no choice but to work leaner, paring down payrolls to only the most essential contributors. As Loren Carlson of the CEO Roundtable somewhat grimly put it, "One of the great benefits of the recession, to some companies, was that they learned how many...employees they could get along without."[1]

But that is only half the story.

On the other side of the employment equation, a countertrend has taken shape: Professionals with portable skills have developed a taste for switching jobs. No longer able safely to rely on a company for sustained employment, they have started relying instead on themselves. Veteran management guru Tom Peters put his finger on the trend when he coined the concept of the "Brand Called You": "You don't 'belong to' any company for life, and your chief affiliation isn't to any particular 'function.' You're not defined by your job title and you're not confined by your job description.... Starting today you are a brand."[2]

With this new freedom, talent no longer have to follow a linear path to be desirable to employers. In fact, those who color outside the lines often appear more attractive to employers and enjoy greater success. My own career path reflects this new approach: By the time I turned 40, I had studied psychology and art history in school, worked for three major global communications networks, been managing partner of a brand consultancy, and even tried my hand as an entrepreneur as a founding partner of a tropical fruit juice company. And while I basically have established a career within the broad confines of marketing, I have friends from college who have cobbled together amazing backgrounds by transferring not just between jobs but also between industries.

As further illustration of this trend away from linearity, I offer the dramatically different career paths of two business superstars: A. G. Lafley and Stephanie Tilenius.

Lafley joined Procter & Gamble upon graduating from Harvard Business School in 1977. After taking a job as a brand assistant for Joy dish soap, he worked his way up the ranks, from brand manager and advertising manager to group vice president, executive vice president, and, ultimately, president, chairman, and CEO before retiring in 2010 and then returning to the helm of the company in 2013.

Like Lafley, Stephanie Tilenius earned an MBA from Harvard Business School—but 19 years later, in 1996. She turned down job offers from investment banking powerhouse Goldman Sachs and from

Microsoft in favor of joining software startup Firefly Network. When that was bought out by Microsoft, she cofounded PlanetRx.com, an online healthcare and e-commerce company, which went public and ultimately fell victim to the bursting of the Internet bubble. Subsequently, Tilenius spent nine years in a variety of positions at eBay, including running eBay Motors, growing PayPal into a multibillion-dollar business, and as senior vice president of eBay.com, before joining Google as vice president of global commerce and payments. In this position, she helped build and launch a variety of products and platforms, including Google Wallet, Google Offers, and Same-Day Delivery. In 2012, she switched gears again and took a job with venture capital firm Kleiner Perkins Caufield & Byers, where she helps late-stage companies in the firm's Digital Growth Fund.

THAT WAS THEN...

A. G. Lafley career path:

1969 – BA, Hamilton College

1977 – MBA, Harvard Business School

1977 – Joined Procter & Gamble as brand assistant, Joy

1978 – Sales training, Denver sales district

1978 – Assistant brand manager, Tide

1980 – Brand manager, Dawn and Ivory Snow

1981 – Brand manager, Special Assignment and Ivory Snow

1982 – Brand manager, Cheer

1983 – Associate advertising manager, PS&D division

1986 – Advertising manager, PS&D division

1988 – General manager, Laundry Products, PS&D division

1991 – Vice president, Laundry and Cleaning Products, Procter & Gamble USA

1992 – Group vice president, the Procter & Gamble Company, and president, Laundry and Cleaning Products, Procter & Gamble USA

1994 – Group vice president, the Procter & Gamble Company, and president, Procter & Gamble Far East

1995 – Executive vice president, the Procter & Gamble Company, and president, Procter & Gamble Asia

1998 – Executive vice president, the Procter & Gamble Company, and president, Procter & Gamble North America

1999 – President, Global Beauty Care and North America

2000 – President and chief executive

2002 – Chairman of the board, president, and chief executive

Source: Procter & Gamble

THIS IS NOW...

Stephanie Tilenius career path:

1990 – Joint BA and MA, Brandeis University

1990 – Presidential Management Intern program (working on trade relations with Japan)

1991 – Technology investment banker, Alex. Brown and Sons

1996 – AOL Inc. (worked in corporate development while in business school)

1996 – MBA, Harvard Business School

1996 – Vice president of product and business development, Firefly Network

1997 – Corporate Business Development Group, Intel Corp.

1997 – Cofounder, PlanetRx.com

2001 – Vice president of International, eBay

2002 – Vice president and general manager, eBay Motors

2003 – Vice president and general manager, PayPal Merchant Services

2008 – Senior vice president, eBay North America and Global Product

2010 – Vice president of global commerce and payments, Google Inc.

2012 – Executive in residence, Kleiner Perkins Caufield & Byers

Source: BusinessWeek

Less than two decades separate the time Lafley and Tilenius spent under the elms at Harvard, but their disparate career paths reflect the sea change in the relationship between employer and employee that we are seeing play out everywhere. The end of jobs for life means companies can easily jettison deadweight. But it also means top talent can shed companies. Even as unemployment levels remain high in many places, businesses are battling it out for the people they need to grow because top recruits are unwilling to sacrifice their own "brands" to prop up companies that are unlikely to get them where they want to go.

Today, a growing number of employers (and employees) are stressing not longevity within a single field but an individual's ability to adapt and learn, which in itself has the potential to grow the business in innovative ways.

TURNING YOUR COMPANY INTO A TALENT MAGNET

The entire talent landscape has changed, and businesses are changing to reflect the new realities. Leadership teams that are serious about developing an innovative, agile company that can reinvent itself as change occurs must be committed to cultivating and developing talent as a core strategic competency. Talent cannot be the focus of the HR department alone; it cannot be a second-order chore palmed off down the chain of command. It must be the top business priority of the most senior people in the company—starting with the CEO. Only through constantly seeking it out, attracting it, motivating it, and fostering a culture to support it will your best asset flourish.

In the process of researching this book, I conducted a survey of more than 100 senior leaders of U.S. companies. Their responses affirmed what I have been seeing and hearing in business generally: Only half are satisfied with the quality of the job candidates available to them—a dismal number in any case but especially at a time when the economy has knocked so many good people out of work. Nearly two-thirds (62 percent) are sufficiently concerned about the talent situations within their

---

Just 50 percent of senior
business leaders surveyed are
satisfied with the quality of job
candidates currently available
to them.

---

organizations that they are making significant changes in how they manage talent. And seven in ten confirmed that C-suite executives are spending more time today on managing talent.[3]

Some speak of a talent shortage. I know from conversations with countless business leaders and HR professionals—and from my own experience—that the talent we need is already out there. All too often, it is being wasted, left unrecognized and underutilized. In the current business environment, we simply cannot afford that.

In the future, the strongest companies will be distinguished by the CEO's hands-on involvement in identifying, grooming, optimizing, and retaining talent. If you are a CEO or a member of the C-suite—or aspire to get there—this book is meant to help you.

The Talent Challenge: Cutting Across Industries

"In my board meetings, talent is front and center. Where I am sitting, the people issue is everything. There is a constant concern about, 'Do we have the best? How do we motivate? What's the pipeline, what's the succession plan?' It is a robust discussion. We are constantly trying to attract people. Talent is critical. Products and services are not enough." —Mellody Hobson, president, Ariel Investments; chairman of the board, DreamWorks Animation SKG

"Talent is a top topic in the C-suite today. There has been a definite uptick in interest. I am astonished at how many jobs companies are trying, without success, to fill. 'How can this be when unemployment is so high?' The problem is, the talent they need is not in great supply. What companies are looking for has changed a lot. And they just end up stealing each other's talent." —David Wilkie, CEO, World 50

"Talent is so important today because it's so thin. If you have a deep bench, you don't worry about your starting players. But if you have no bench, talent

is everything. And we have decades of American industry gutting itself. They have almost completely eliminated research and development, and that has alienated the smart tech brains. We have no depth. It's gauze protecting us, not chain mail." —Robert X. Cringely, technology journalist and author of Accidental Empires

"Building the plants and shipping the stuff, that's the easy part. The hard part is getting the right talent. Talent is the tip of the spear. You can build the most beautiful plant in the middle of China, and if you don't have the right people, it will be a mausoleum." —Carlos Abrams-Rivera, senior vice president, marketing, Mondelēz International

In the next two chapters, I explore a number of significant workplace shifts—some with roots in the technology industry and others being propelled by a new generation and an emerging mindset—before setting out the six essential strategies every forward-thinking company will need to embrace to come out on top.

QUESTIONS TO ASK YOURSELF

- Talent likely accounts for the bulk of your company's expense base. Are the time and care allotted to it commensurate with that level of importance?
- What role do your senior executives play in attracting, engaging, motivating, and retaining top talent? Where are the dangerous points of weakness?
- Where does the underutilized talent lie within your organization—and what needs to happen to unlock that value?

CHAPTER 2

SILICON VALLEY

BIRTHPLACE OF THE TALENT REVOLUTION

IT IS HARDLY A NEWSFLASH THAT WE HAVE BEEN LIVING through a vast technological upheaval that has changed our lives profoundly. The crucible of this phenomenon is, of course, Silicon Valley, a place that, just a few decades ago, was known mostly for apple farming. At that time it was simply Santa Clara Valley. And it was here amid scrubby fields and rattlesnakes that Bill Hewlett and Dave Packard famously set up shop in a tiny garage in 1939. In another garage on a suburban driveway, Steve Jobs and Steve Wozniak assembled their first computer, the Apple I, in 1976. A little more than two decades later, Larry Page and Sergey Brin founded Google in yet another garage.

For the first-time visitor, the Valley's balmy climate, palm trees, and casual dress might suggest little more than just another laid-back vacation destination. That is, until you see the road signs bearing some familiar names: Google, Apple, eBay, Intel, Oracle, Cisco. This relatively unassuming 1,500 square miles in Northern California accounts for an astonishing 40 percent of all the venture capital investment in the United States.

(The United States, in turn, accounts for around 70 percent of global investment.)

Out of all those humble garages dotting the Valley have sprung technological breakthroughs the impact of which has yet to be fathomed fully. To describe them requires the use of numbers formerly reserved for talking about the vast reaches of interstellar space: At present, there are more than one billion smartphones all over the planet, with another billion coming by 2015; the Internet has more than 13 billion web pages, their total data measured in terabytes; YouTube (founded not in a garage but in an apartment above a pizzeria) now has more than one billion users, rivaling Facebook. And those are just a few of the most widely recognized examples.

What interests me about the region within the context of this book, however, is not its product output but its talent input. As staggering as all this technological change has been, Silicon Valley has given the world a second—and, I would argue, an equally profound—legacy: It is the birthplace of the talent revolution. While originally seen as an outlier in the business of talent management, the Valley has emerged as a pioneering force in setting the bar for how modern companies manage talent and, more generally, for how they operate...and even think.

For this reason, I made it a point to spend time with some of the leading companies there. I wanted to see what I could learn and what lessons I could apply to my own company. I expected to discover a lot I didn't know about talent, but I ended up being simply blown away—not just by how cultures can be built, maintained, and grown, but also by what happens when you authentically put people first, when you unreservedly place talent at the core of your business thinking.

Many of the ideas I will be discussing in this book originated, in one way or another—or at least have been most artfully practiced—in the Valley. They may have started out as fringe concepts formulated by shaggy geeks munching on day-old pizza, but they are accepted best practices today at such old-line giants and people-first practitioners as Unilever, Goldman Sachs, and McKinsey & Company. At the start of our exploration of today's reshaped talent landscape, I will focus on three of these ideas—each one a fundamental practice of smart companies that put people first:

- Push decision making downward
- Flatten the organization
- Promote continuous learning

PUSH DECISION MAKING DOWNWARD

An early glimmer of the talent revolution appeared at Hewlett-Packard (HP), with its radical reinvention of corporate management. Decentralized decision making was a key feature of "the HP Way." Perhaps it was the California sunshine that encouraged a new, liberated way of thinking about the workplace. Perhaps it was the great distance from the stodgy East Coast centers of corporate-think. Or perhaps it was the high percentage of Mensa-worthy IQs among the HP ranks. Whatever the reasons, the company thought very differently about how employee and employer should interact.

From the start, Silicon Valley workers were independent minded, often described as embodying the cowboy spirit of the West. Their loyalty to a boss was far less than their loyalty to their personal dreams, so confident were they of their own abilities and promise. Nobel Prize winner and transistor pioneer William Shockley found this out the hard way: In 1956, he set up a lab near Palo Alto and hired some brilliant young researchers. The next year, eight of those employees—tired of the boss's high-handed management style and unhappy with his decision not to continue researching silicon-based semiconductors—quit their jobs and established Fairchild Semiconductor, which ended up pioneering integrated circuits and leaving their old employer in the dust.

One of these so-called traitorous eight was Gordon Moore, who went on to cofound Intel. For this new company, he adopted innovative practices such as everyone calling co-workers by their first names and having staff work in cubicles rather than closed offices. Reflecting on his experiences in a 1996 interview, Moore voiced an early insight that ran totally counter to standard hierarchical thinking back in the Eisenhower era—and still does even now for all too many laggard companies. Moore said that, in a fast-developing business, the people with the power are the people who understand what is going on, and these people are not necessarily at the top. At Intel, Moore set things up so that the workers who had the knowledge were charged with making decisions, with each given virtually equal say.[1]

This perceptive idea was destined to have an explosive impact on the history of U.S. business. In countless conversations as I researched this book, I heard corporate leaders describe how, more and more, they are empowering their midlevel employees to make their own decisions, to follow their own initiatives, with far less top-down command and control than had been the rule in years past. In fact, only around one in ten of the business leaders we surveyed believe that command-and-control structures are still the best way to get value from their workers.[2]

> **Only 11 percent of senior business leaders surveyed agree that "command-and-control structures are still the best approach to getting the most value from employees."**

This shift in attitude is being helped along by new technologies that allow workers in the middle tier to have instant access to vast amounts of data—data that previously were restricted to the upper echelons. In addition, technology has provided tools that greatly empower individual workers as thinking, decision-making, creative forces. These factors have swelled the Intel model of decades ago into a tsunami sweeping through today's global workplace, empowering talent across a broad spectrum within each company—with the concomitant overall result that talent matters today more than it ever has before.

FLATTEN THE ORGANIZATION

Many Americans first woke up to the existence of Silicon Valley by watching a TV commercial. It aired in prime time only once, on January

22, 1984, and lasted just 60 seconds—but its ramifications have been far-reaching. I am referring, of course, to the celebrated Super Bowl ad promoting the Apple Macintosh. Who could forget the menacing Big Brother addressing, by giant screen, a room full of cowering and slack-jawed worker-drones? Into this monochromatic throng runs a colorfully dressed young athlete who hurls a hammer and destroys the image of Big Brother, which dissolves in a shower of sparks.

Most of the audience knew full well that Big Brother was a reference to "Big Blue"—to IBM, the company that dominated the computer market all those years ago—while Apple was the hammer-wielding voice of nonconformity and revolution. But from today's perspective, the ad takes on added resonance, symbolizing what Silicon Valley was about to do to the American workforce in general: liberating many a worker-drone and smashing the old paradigms forever.

The Valley's approach to talent management, stressing the autonomy of the individual and an eradication of hierarchies, truly opened the way for today's talent revolution. From the moment that 1984 commercial aired, one could argue, the old management models of corporate America were doomed—for what company would want to invite ridicule by clinging to a discredited approach that favored authoritarian control by harsh and seldom-seen autocrats? With that visionary commercial, Apple was not just selling a product; it was directly challenging an entire culture of command-and-control corporate conformism.

Within a few years, organizations everywhere had begun to flatten, a trend that would rapidly accelerate in the twenty-first century as the information technology (IT) earthquake reshaped every aspect of how we do business. In my sector, an industry in which, on average, 60 percent of our total costs are our people, we have come to learn the value of engaging smaller teams in a "garage-like" mindset to get the job done. Last summer at Arnold Worldwide, a micronetwork (16 agencies in 15 countries) that is part of the Havas family, we built the new global, responsively designed Jack Daniels website—a site that cleverly adapts to whatever device it is viewed on, whether a desktop, tablet, or mobile. From the initial concept through to launch, we built the site in only 15 weeks across 30 countries—with a team of just six people. It is amazing what can be accomplished with a clear mandate, an agile team, and a flattened structure.

PROMOTE CONTINUOUS LEARNING

The hammer-throwing woman in the "1984" ad was obviously a thinking being—as contrasted with the brainwashed zombies whose minds she sought to reawaken. And here, too, Silicon Valley was destined to push all of American business in a new direction: toward emphasizing the worker not as a cog in the wheel but rather as an intelligent, unique individual who, with proper attention and training, can offer ever-increasing levels of value in the teeming ideas economy.

Today's tremendous new stress on continuous learning is one of the most valuable legacies handed down from the Valley. The centrality of Stanford University may account for part of the reason that learning has always been considered so essential there; but then again, it may also be the fact that so many tech luminaries dropped out of school to start learning by following their personal ambitions: Bill Gates and Steve Ballmer of Microsoft, Mark Zuckerberg of Facebook, Larry Ellison of Oracle, Michael Dell, and, of course, Steve Jobs.

At a Stanford commencement address in 2005, Jobs described how dropping out of Reed College in Oregon freed him up to take classes in subjects that especially interested him—a calligraphy course, for example, that eventually enabled him to design elegant typography into Apple computers, thereby helping to create a powerful competitive advantage. In an interview a decade prior, Jobs stressed broad-minded learning as a key ingredient at Apple: "I think part of what made the Macintosh great was that the people working on it were musicians and poets and artists and zoologists and historians who also happened to be the best computer scientists in the world."[3]

In Valley culture, continuous learning is about a lot more than taking classes and having established expertise, though; it is fundamentally about trying new things, paying attention to what happens, and feeding the observations back into the next round—somewhat like evolution and natural selection. In Silicon Valley, and increasingly everywhere else, no company and no individual can afford to think that they have achieved the definitive version of anything; there will always be competitors figuring out smarter alternatives. Continuous learning is not just a nice-to-have extra for quality of life. Today it is vital for survival. This notion underpins that most famous Apple mantra, stressing the centrality of mental agility and having a broad perspective: Think Different.

As we start to think differently about the world of talent today, we will encounter many references to Silicon Valley. That sunbaked region represents the vital hearth for the revolutionary ideas we will be considering—ideas that have, as much as any microchip, transformed the working world.

QUESTIONS TO ASK YOURSELF

- Is your business suited to a garage—not in terms of physical space and infrastructure, but in terms of being willing to take chances, rely on your instincts, and push ahead even when you are going against conventional wisdom?
- What more could you be doing to empower your bright midlevel employees to make decisions on their own?
- Have you flattened the organization, or do traces of top-down authoritarianism hamper your talent's creative freedom? Where can current hierarchies be compressed or removed altogether?
- How are you ensuring that your talent pool is learning new things every day? What opportunities and motivations have you built into your structure to foster continuous learning?

CHAPTER 3

A NEW WAY TO WORK

THE REVOLUTION IN THE WORKPLACE THAT IS CURRENTLY under way is heavily influenced by Silicon Valley, as we have seen, but it is also driven in part by the millennials—our newest generation of talent—and those who think like them. We are seeing the emergence of a distinctive set of attitudes, behaviors, and skills that are reshaping our entire approach to work. This change is happening for a reason: The old ways of working are neither sufficiently nimble nor sufficiently speedy to accomplish all that we need to in the new century. We have no choice but to adapt.

A GENERATION *AND* A MINDSET

The new attitudes and behaviors extend across age groups, but they are most apparent among millennials. Virtually everyone I spoke with in the course of writing this book had strong opinions about millennials—mostly positive but occasionally quite biting. Several made the point that millennials, like all generations, fall within a spectrum; in their case, from stereotypically overindulged whiners with an outsized sense of entitlement to the tremendously ambitious and entrepreneurial go-getters who are starting their own

---

By 2025, millennials will account for three out of every four workers globally.

---

businesses at an age when most of us were still lugging our school books around campus. The vast majority fall somewhere in between.

What matters foremost to those of us who run businesses is that millennials will soon make up the bulk of our workforces. They constitute around one-third of the U.S. population and, by 2025, will account for three out of every four workers globally. With baby boomers retiring and not enough generation Xers to take their place, companies will have no choice but to tap this new generation's teeming reserves.

Millennials will have a dramatic and lasting impact on the way we work for a number of reasons: First, they are innately collaborative, accustomed to working in teams and co-creating with friends and strangers halfway across the world. They expect to continue to do so in their careers. Second, as digital natives, they tend to have little patience for anyone who has yet to embrace the latest technological gadgetry. And third, they are a generation that rejects formality and hierarchy in favor of approaches that are, like, far more casual and egalitarian—whether it be in their language, their choices of clothing at work, or how they prefer to interact with colleagues.

As the millennial masses wash over us, businesses are working hard to attract, absorb, and make the most of this new breed of talent. It is already abundantly clear that millennials do not intend to mold themselves into the existing culture the way previous cohorts did. In fact, their whole approach to work is disruptive to the established ways of doing things. And from what I have been seeing, when the millennial mindset comes up against corporate customs, it is the latter that end up giving way.

KEY SHIFTS THAT WILL TRANSFORM HOW WE WORK

In this chapter, we'll consider a few of the macro changes that are part of what I call the millennial mindset:

- The new emphasis on values and paychecks with a purpose
- The growing insistence on a more sustainable work-life integration
- The ascendency of free agency
- The embrace of all things digital

All these characteristics are increasingly found among talent of all ages but are particularly prevalent within the up-and-coming generation.

PAYCHECKS WITH A PURPOSE

In Steve Jobs's 2005 commencement address at Stanford, he counseled the young graduates to do what they love: "Your work," he said, "is going to fill a large part of your life, and the only way to be truly satisfied is to do what you believe is great work. And the only way to do great work is to love what you do. If you haven't found it yet, keep looking. Don't settle."[1]

Our newest generation of talent has taken that advice to heart—advice they no doubt have heard repeated throughout their lifetimes by baby boomer parents disillusioned with the careers they have "settled" into. In a 2012 study by MTV, half of millennials surveyed said they would "rather have no job than have a job they hate."[2] Among the top factors that shape job desirability, "loving what I do" beat out both salary and big bonuses. Similarly, research by Capstrat in 2011 found that 72 percent of millennials would be willing to sacrifice a higher salary for a more fulfilling career.[3]

It is not that people no longer care about salary and the other traditional trappings of success, it is just that they want more than that—more meaning, more opportunity to make a measurable difference (inside and, oftentimes, outside the company), more reason to take pride in what they do every day. And we are seeing this attitude take hold across many industries, from startups to long-established corporations.

Henry Sauer is in charge of talent and human resources at Rackspace, a fast-growing tech company housed in a former shopping mall in San

Antonio, Texas. The company specializes in cloud computing. Sauer told me that the people at Rackspace "want to work in a place that lines up with their values and where they can pursue something beyond themselves and that is meaningful to the world." In a similar vein, Michele Buck, a senior vice president at a more traditional company—famed chocolate maker Hershey in Pennsylvania—noted that prospective hires are showing a heightened interest in the company's long legacy of philanthropy. They want to work at a place whose values they share: "That matters much more now," she said.

When I look at the companies within Havas Worldwide that perform best—and at our client partners whose businesses do the best—they share the common DNA of commitment to strong values and putting people first. Whatever the industry, employers that offer their people a sense of meaning and prioritize the people whose lives they touch are going to have an edge.

WORK-LIFE INTEGRATION

When I was a kid, nine to five was the standard workday. Our parents left home around the hour we were heading out to school, and, for the most part, they returned in time for dinner. Weekends were family time. Sounds quaint, doesn't it? Since the 1990s, the delineation between life and work has grown far less distinct, as work hours have been extended and new technologies have let us bring the office with us wherever we go. We answer emails while sitting on the sidelines at our children's soccer games, and we take work calls in parking lots outside restaurants and while on vacation. We are never truly disengaged from the workplace.

Despite these many changes, those of us over the age of 40 still tend to think of the traditional work-time hours as off-limits for personal use. We feel a twinge of guilt when we update our Facebook statuses or indulge in a little online shopping while at the office. For us, the workday remains somehow sacrosanct—we are at work to do what we are paid for. Period. But for millennials, and those who think like them, this hardly holds true anymore.

The younger generation enjoys what is probably an all-around healthier relationship with work—although an enormously frustrating one, at times, to certain older colleagues and bosses. Millennials, on the whole, expect flexibility and see no reason to adhere to a formal schedule that prevents them from making optimal use of their hours. The MTV study I mentioned earlier found that 81 percent of millennials—versus 69 percent of baby boomers—think they should be allowed to devise their own hours at work. Nearly nine in ten want the workplace to be social and fun, and 70 percent said they need "me time" on the job. Three out of five college students surveyed by Cisco said they have a *right* to work remotely and with a flexible schedule.[4]

At Timberland, vice president of global marketing Jim Davey marvels at the distinctively millennial attitudes now emerging. "We spent more than a year talking to millennials around the world, and some clear patterns emerged. In particular, they're looking for a much greater balance between life and work—they've seen that the brass ring may not be there at the end, so they want a good balance of life throughout the journey."

Rather than scoff at such notions, companies across industries are signaling that they are sympathetic to this longing for a more balanced approach. "Workplace flexibility is very important and has been for some time. The younger generation has been more vocal than previous generations about this need, indicating that flexibility is no longer a 'nice to have' but rather an expectation of employees," says Chris Benko, vice president of global talent management at Merck. "They want to work for companies that will allow them to do what they need to do in order to balance work and family. Senior leaders who incorporate this into their own schedules and who talk openly about flexibility in the workplace send the signal, 'This is OK.'"

FREE AGENCY

Earlier I mentioned the move away from lifelong employment and toward a more eclectic approach to career building. Younger workers are taking this trend to new heights, with more than nine in ten expecting to stay in their current job for less than three years.[5] A 2010 study by Intrepid found that the average number of jobs a person now has by age 26 is seven.[6] At the rate they are going, they will surely have 20 or more jobs in their lifetimes.

In a remarkable reversal of traditional practice, it has even become faddish to collect companies on one's resume, so to speak. Marty St. George, senior vice president of marketing and commercial at JetBlue, described to me, in some perplexity, a young employee in business development who "loved it here, but resigned to go to another employer because she wanted more companies on her resume. Younger employees see it as all part of life's adventure."

The lure of entrepreneurship is also particularly strong among this generation. More than one-third of employed millennials have started their own businesses on the side to supplement their incomes.[7] Talent legend Dan Walker, long at Apple (under Steve Jobs), at Gap Inc. (under retail guru Mickey Drexler), and now founder and CEO of talent advisory group The Human Revolution Studios, told me what he is seeing: "Brilliant young engineers today are not going to Google or Apple, but starting their own companies. Instagram—that was 13 bright young people with a simple but brilliant product. They stole Facebook's most critical core customer, America's youth, in a matter of months because Facebook was too complex, and their mothers and grandmothers were using it. Instagram was efficient and cool; Facebook wasn't. Mark Zuckerberg had no choice but to buy them out for $715 million." Millennials know such stories all too well, and many are inspired to follow suit.

How are companies dealing with the new restlessness, the increasing propensity to jump ship? Certainly, they have to work much harder to enhance workplace culture and give young people a reason to stay. Stephanie Tilenius—former vice president at eBay and Google and now with venture capital firm Kleiner Perkins Caufield & Byers— summarizes the situation: "New college graduates have very different perspectives on the workforce. In the old days you stayed a long time, in a kind of indentured servitude; you worked your way up, and there were hierarchies. Today, the average tenure in Silicon Valley is two years. There is this view that you prioritize yourself first, learn skills, and you move on: 'What am I going to get out of it?' Now actually, this is potentially a good thing; it raises the bar for companies." Rackspace's Henry Sauer agrees: "With the influx of millennials into the workforce, who are not attached to the company forever and want more out of life than just a paycheck, companies have got to create a compelling environment and mission for their employees. They have to be a place where people can learn and grow."

Businesses also have to discard antiquated notions of progression timelines. I have worked closely with Matt Howell, chief digital officer at Havas Creative Group. As he sees it, the Internet "has created a much more meritocratic environment. In the past, the ascent up the corporate ladder was measured in *time*. There was an unstated contract that there was a time-based progression. But with digital, most of our recruits have never worked in an ad agency. They worked in software companies or startups where tenure and age, formal training, have very little to do with anything. Now it's, 'Can you handle the task, or not?'" So, I asked him, how should a company respond to these new conditions? "What we are trying to do at our agencies," says Howell, "is flatten organizational structures so younger people can contribute at much younger ages. Rewarding ability not experience." Another reminder of the long arm of Silicon Valley culture.

DIGITAL NATIVES

Technological multitasking is widely flagged as a signature trait of the millennial generation—whiz kids simultaneously texting, gaming, watching a sitcom, and IM'ing on Facebook, even as they are at their desks working for you. Their ability to do all this successfully strikes some as unnatural, and some older folks are convinced that millennials' minds are actually different from ours, given that these young people have been steeped in digital from the time they were in diapers. In a 2011 Pew survey, a majority of respondents agreed that "the brains of multitasking teens and young adults are 'wired' differently from those over age 35 and overall it yields helpful results."[8]

This wired existence means that many millennials (and older talent who have embraced the digital work style) are perfectly happy interacting electronically instead of in person. And they are less likely to have patience for the endless meetings to which the rest of us have become wearily accustomed. Deborah Borg, vice president of human resources at chemical giant Dow, says this difference in perspective is already being felt in the workplace: "Younger workers are less concerned with face-to-face. Their attitude is 'Give me technology and let me connect with people'; they are much more willing to form strong relationships through online tools."

For veteran marketer Mark Bergsrud, "The only thing that is hard for me with millennials is getting used to the way they want to work. You cannot see them face-to-face as often as you would like. But with the technology, they do get the work done." Speaking of his time at United Airlines, Bergsrud adds, "A lot of our employees had better technology at home than they did at work"—designers with bigger monitors, for example—but he cautioned them about too much shunning of human contact. To move up in the company, "you need face time and relationships," he says, not an existence spent sequestered with a screen.

The use of social media in the workplace is also a growing issue at many companies. A 2011 study by Cisco found that two in three college students regularly ask about social media policies during job interviews, and 56 percent will either refuse to accept an offer from a company that bans social media or simply plan to circumvent the policy once hired.[9]

Each of the above characteristics—demand for work with a purpose, work-life integration, free agency, and digital everything—is contributing to today's fast-changing business landscape. Together, they are pushing the modern company in directions far removed from the familiar workplaces of the twentieth century. We may sometimes fear these changes, but we need to accept and even encourage them if we are going to grow and thrive in an altered world.

Millennials as Promise and Challenge

Formerly with American Express and Aetna, Belinda Lang is one of today's top marketers. "Millennials are great," she told me enthusiastically. "They have more of a pulse on what's going on, what's new in the marketplace. A fresher approach to business. I see openness, a willingness to ask questions and to challenge; it is really refreshing if channeled the right way. And they want to be part of an organization with a purpose. Some older workers are just happy to have a job!"

I asked if today's schools are providing adequate skills. She replied, "No. Millennials need to learn how to go to the office. They need a lot of coaching and mentoring. To learn how to write an email and not say, 'Hey' to everybody, to superiors."

To Lang, millennials are brimming with potential but come with a difficult challenge: "My biggest question is this: I see a lot of very young, entrepreneurial, talented people who are much more likely than previous generations to want to go out on their own, to create their own businesses. What keeps them long-term engaged and motivated to stay in a large corporation?"

QUESTIONS TO ASK YOURSELF

- How well has your company adapted itself to derive the most value from the newest generation of workers—and all those who have adopted a millennial mindset?
- What sense of purpose do you offer talent beyond the numbers they see on their paystubs?
- What are you doing to afford your talent a healthier integration of life and work?
- What flexibility has been built into your processes to enable people to work in the manner that best suits them?
- What more could you do to encourage cross-generational collaboration and learning?

PART II

SIX ESSENTIAL STRATEGIES FOR SUCCESS

All of us seek to gain competitive advantages for our businesses. And there is no better way to do this than to improve the talent equation. The heart of this book consists of specific recommendations designed to help you transform your talented workers into enthusiastic superstars eager to perform for you, every day. Looking toward the future, these approaches seem highly promising:

Strategy One: *Cultivate Your Culture*
Strategy Two: *Don't Manage...Lead!*
Strategy Three: *Live What's Next*
Strategy Four: *Create a Sense of Dynamism*
Strategy Five: *Be People-Centric*
Strategy Six: *Make It Mean Something*

STRATEGY ONE

CULTIVATE YOUR CULTURE

CHAPTER 4

ATTEND TO
YOUR DNA

*You can replicate what a company does, but not its culture—that has
become a business's biggest differentiator and advantage.*
                    —Deborah Borg, vice president, human resources,
                                        Dow Chemical Company

AS I WALK THE HALLS HERE AT THE HAVAS WORLDWIDE
headquarters in New York, I see employees engaged in all
kinds of activities in this ceaselessly busy hive. As with any
large company, you will find a mix of individuals, from our corporate
data analysts wearing the traditional work-casual khakis and button-
downs to our junior copywriters wearing the trendiest SoHo looks.
Their jobs vary enormously, as do their personal styles, backgrounds,
and skill sets—but what ties them all together into an organic whole is
that all-but-indefinable thing called *culture*. It is something we all value
highly... and something I want to help shape and develop, both for the
immediate benefits and because of the impact it will have on our brand.
I have never worked at a company that had a strong culture that did
not do well; I have, however, worked at companies where the opposite
was true.

I will touch only briefly on the complicated subject of corporate culture, but I would be remiss not to note that it forms a tremendously important piece of the new talent puzzle. In the last couple of decades, it has gone from being something discussed primarily in dry academic journals to a key criterion that prospective employees evaluate as they make their job choices.

Although there have been company cultures for centuries, the term *corporate culture* typically brings to mind the 1955 novel *The Man in the Gray Flannel Suit* and a stifling kind of hyperconformity. That is a bad form of culture, obviously. At the other end of the spectrum, we think of Silicon Valley culture, which evokes images of catered carts of gourmet hummus and ahi tuna, balance ball chairs, and foosball tournaments at three in the morning. Beyond these stereotypes are the real cultures that we see in organizations everywhere—cultures that exert such a powerful effect on business outcomes that more than one observer has concluded that "culture eats strategy for lunch."[1]

There is something strangely intangible about culture, something that can be felt but not always articulated. As David Wilkie, chief executive of World 50, says, "Culture is what happens when you are not looking." It transmits its subtle influences by word of mouth and everyday interactions; it is "what people say about your company to their friends. The way associates treat each other and treat the customers."

For better or worse, every business has a culture, just as every geographical locale has one. From the perspective of employees, culture is everything experienced in their interactions with the organization: the visual impressions, the sounds, the vibe they pick up at every touch point—it is the way they are spoken to, the way they are encouraged and cajoled or browbeaten and harassed. It is what makes some

"Company culture is the ambient feeling of what is right and what is wrong. An unwritten principle or covenant about right and wrong." —Alexis Nasard, Heineken N.V.

workplaces a pleasure to go to and others a source of dread as Monday morning draws near.

From the perspective of consumers, culture is the all-around experience they have in their dealings with a company. It is the whole package of intangibles that makes people happy to do business with culture-driven outfits such as Southwest Airlines, Whole Foods, and Zappos and to cease doing business with other companies that have failed to master the human touch.

More and more CEOs are getting hands-on about culture. Dan Gill is cofounder and chief executive of Huddler, which creates sophisticated platforms for online discussion-forum sites. He admits to having been slow to put culture first, there being so many urgent tasks associated with founding a company. Initially, he told me, "We just put our heads down and got work done. Only later did we codify what was important in being at Huddler. We formed a Culture Corps to define what makes being at Huddler great, what we aspired to be, and to reinforce both going forward."

I am convinced that a carefully cultivated culture will be central to the most prosperous businesses in the future. And the senior business leaders I surveyed for this book feel the same: 97 percent agreed strongly or somewhat that "a strong culture can be a company's most valuable asset."[2] Everywhere I look, I see ambitious leaders now intent on getting their cultures right, looking to companies they admire for tips on fine-tuning their own cultures or even trying to overhaul a dysfunctional culture that is holding the company back. Already, culture is shooting up the ranks of what people care about in any company. Compensation still matters, of course, but culture is often a critical determinant in whether talent will join, stay, or go.

Yes, cultures vary enormously, but the best of them seem to share

> Ninety-seven percent of senior business leaders surveyed agree: "A strong culture can be a company's most valuable asset."

certain common denominators. In judging your company's culture, you might ask yourself these questions:

1. Is the culture grounded in values?
2. Does the culture promote cohesion?
3. Does the CEO make culture a top priority?

IS THE CULTURE GROUNDED IN VALUES?

Paul Polman is chief executive officer of consumer goods giant Unilever and one of today's most universally respected business leaders. I spoke with him at Unilever House in London about the critical role that values play in building businesses. "Values are the underlying truth that defines who we all are and who we want to be," he said. "Without values, there is no basis for trust." So important are its values to the company that Unilever celebrates them each year with a Heroes program that "highlights people from around the world who live our values." In 2012, five people were honored in this way for contributions that ranged from helping the company progress toward its sustainability goals to redesigning a tool used in tea harvesting. Each honoree contributed in some way to Unilever's overarching purpose of helping people "feel good, look good, and get more out of life."

You might find it useful to think of values as your culture's DNA. In the human body, DNA is present in every cell and acts as a dynamic blueprint that essentially tells the body what to do and how to grow. In a business culture, values do much the same thing: They tell the culture what to do and what not to do, and they guide future development. The keyword here is *do*; values have no meaning until they are translated into action. And values statements are just idle chatter unless we actively live by them. Never forget that one of the darkest chapters in U.S. corporate history was written by a company that trumpeted its dedication to its lofty values. On the marbled lobby walls of its Houston headquarters, energy firm Enron boasted of its commitment to "Communication,

Respect, Integrity, and Excellence." It even developed a 64-page code of ethics manual. But the actions of Enron's leaders—and the behaviors they rewarded—were ludicrously out of whack with the values they espoused, and the company imploded, taking lots of people down with it, in 2004.

ORGANIZATIONAL COMPASS AND GLUE

One benefit of having clearly defined and adhered-to values is that it simplifies and speeds up business decisions. Reflecting on running Southwest Airlines according to a simple set of values, cofounder Herb Kelleher told *Fortune* magazine, "If somebody makes a proposal and it infringes on those values, you don't study it for two years. You just say, 'No, we don't do that.' And you go on quickly. So I think that contributes to efficiency."[3] In enormous companies spread across many locations, values can also serve as a shared lingua franca, a kind of organizational glue.

Developing a company culture for a business with a single location, where employees know their leaders and regularly see them living out the values, is relatively simple. It is far more difficult to develop a culture for a business that has thousands of employees spread across territories and harder still to maintain one company culture when businesses merge. A primary reason that the 2001 merger of Time Warner and AOL bombed is that the two organizations' cultures and values proved incompatible. Insufficient attention was paid to identifying shared values and aligning the cultures around them.

Fostering a shared culture and values was a major focus for Kraft Foods Inc., which split into two entities in October 2012: Kraft Foods Group Inc. and Mondelēz International Inc. The latter is a world leader in chocolate, biscuits, gum, candy, coffee, and powdered beverages, with billion-dollar brands such as Cadbury chocolate; Jacobs coffee; LU, Nabisco, and Oreo biscuits; Tang powdered beverages, and Trident gum. As senior vice president of marketing Carlos Abrams-Rivera tells it, becoming crystal clear about seven key values helped knit the new company together: "These are the things we believe are important to us and how we operate," he says. "They shape our DNA as a new company.

MONDELĒZ INTERNATIONAL

Our Values Guide Us
Inspire trust.
Act like owners.
Keep it simple.
Be open and inclusive.
Tell it like it is.
Lead from the head and
the heart.
Discuss. Decide. Deliver.

We selected the best elements of the companies in creating a cohesive culture. Our intention is to use the values not as a pretty picture for the world, but in making decisions about how we run the business. We are committed to certain financial goals, but also to how we deliver them."

INCREASED RECRUITING POWER

A strong culture and values are not just about what you do internally; they are also a key aspect in how you are seen by the world. And that means so much more at a time when competition for talent is exception-

> **Ninety-four percent of senior business leaders agree: "Companies with clear values have an edge in recruiting top candidates."**

ally ferocious. Nearly all the senior leaders we surveyed for this book (94 percent) agreed, "Companies with clear values have an edge in recruiting top candidates."[4] There is nothing fuzzy about that.

ROLLING OUT OUR VISION AND VALUES AT ARNOLD WORLDWIDE

Across Havas, I have found that our best companies are those that not only have a clearly articulated vision but also have the values necessary to support that vision. When we engineered the turnaround at Arnold Worldwide, this was critical. Arnold was suffering from being a company that relied on what had made it great in the past. But the world had moved on quickly, and we weren't moving fast enough. We needed not just to get everyone aligned around where we were headed but also to create a belief system—and a behavioral-operating system—to get us there. It was not easy.

One of the most important pieces to rolling out our defined vision and values was making sure our talent was intrinsically involved from the get-go. The actual words came from our people. The agency

ARNOLD WORLDWIDE

Our Vision: **To be the most pro-gressive agency, where brilliant creativity meets technology, delivering game-changing ideas for our clients.**

Our Values:

- **Proactive: Thinking ahead + Taking action**
- **Evolving: Committed to growth + Always learning**
- **Daring: Pushing boundaries + Challenging convention**
- **Connected: Plugged in + Informed**
- **Open: Respectful + Interested**

leadership hosted roundtables made up of employees from all levels and departments and engaged them in conversation about what they loved about Arnold, what they hated, what was working, and what wasn't. The words and the sentiments from each close up (round table) informed how the vision and values were written.

Having so many people involved in the development process gave us a bit of a head start when it came to rolling out the final result. That said, it was just the beginning. Our roll-out plan was split into four phases:

1. Awareness: "I know what the vision and values are, and I know where to find out more."
2. Understanding: "I know why we're doing this. I've seen examples."
3. Ownership: "I know how to make a difference. I want to do this."
4. Engagement: "I believe in the vision and values. I'm living and breathing them."

In the awareness and understanding phases, I joined with other members of the Arnold board in hosting another set of roundtables—first with leaders and then with the rest of the agency. There, I explained in detail how the vision and values were developed, what they meant to the agency, and where employees could expect to see their impact. Particular atten-tion was paid to making sure that leaders understood, were on board, and were able to talk to their people about it. I also explained that as time went on (as we reached the ownership and engagement phases), employ-ees should expect to be held accountable to adhering to those values and making decisions in line with the vision.

More specifically, the way in which Arnold Worldwide evaluated talent was about to change radically. We were revamping our entire performance review process and creating a progress review instead. In line with the company's vision "to be the most progressive," we designed a custom process that focuses on ongoing feedback and coaching rather than a once-per-year assessment against past performance. The new process includes specific steps throughout the year in which the entire agency engages simultaneously. And, in what is possibly the biggest change for Arnold, the process now includes an evaluation against key attributes, largely made up of the company values. Including the values in progress reviews ensures that the vision and values are a topic of conversation throughout the year, every year.

DOES THE CULTURE PROMOTE COHESION?

Founded by three programmers in 2003, The Nerdery Interactive Labs is a cutting-edge IT company in Minneapolis. It needs a high percentage of top tech talent, and so it has built its culture around being "the best place for programmers to work." In this vibrant workplace, perks abound: In addition to being a dog-friendly zone, the company maintains a perpetual chess tournament and boasts a 250-seat rock-band venue, 15 employee clubs, arcade games, Photoshop contests, comic books in the lobby, and *Star Trek* memorabilia in the conference room. But don't mistake perks or décor for the really substantive part of what makes The Nerdery a great place to work: its ability to instill a family-like ethos—supportive, friendly, and cohesive.

"Perks are not culture," says Kris Szafranski, director of organizational change. What really matters is how the company treats people: "You have individual attention here. Someone is looking out for you and working to make you better. A lot of places write code; the difference is in how we treat each other." He stresses that "perks, we can survive without. The culture, we cannot." That strong, family-like culture is helping The Nerdery win the talent war for programmers and developers. The company has grown from 38 employees in 2006 (the year Szafranski came on board) to 440 as of mid-2013. And revenues between 2006 and 2012 soared from $2.5 million to $37.1 million.

CREATING A JOYFUL AND GENUINE CULTURE AT BEN & JERRY'S

Walt Freese knows more than almost anyone about how to make culture a top priority: He was long the chief executive of Ben & Jerry's and subsequently was CEO of yogurt maker Stonyfield Farm. The famously positive culture at the former was evident in the cohesion of the people employed there and also by the lengths to which the company went to make every day a good one. For starters, there was the Joy Gang (charged with motivating and entertaining staff), a slide in the Treehouse conference room, a health and fitness center with trainers, on-site massage, and a nap room. As a result of these and other measures, Freese says proudly, "Our employee culture became more and more engaged and joyful. Unwanted turnover was virtually zero, and we doubled the business. Now that would never have happened without changes in the way we thought about talent and culture. It's all about doing an excellent job on culture and employee development and mission and values—and fun and irreverence."

Freese adds, "I strove to create a culture where people didn't need to park any part of themselves at the door, especially not their hearts and souls. I believe deeply that the success of any company is tied directly to the quality of its talent and its ability to utilize that talent. And that is where culture comes in: It allows you to create an environment in which you can effectively utilize talent."

He emphasized a deeper purpose as well: "At Ben & Jerry's, everybody knew they were there to create a great brand, to run a great business, but also to change the world in the process. They felt they were on a mission. This engages people in a way few other things can in business. Employees said to me, 'It's easy to find another job, but it's hard to find another company like this one.'"

DOES THE CEO MAKE CULTURE A TOP PRIORITY?

There are three or four things the CEO simply must get right. One of them is culture.

—John Ciancutti, director of engineering, Facebook

As discussed earlier, all organizations have a culture, regardless of whether anybody is paying attention to it. It is what inevitably develops when a bunch of *Homo sapiens* regularly spend time together. Sometimes great cultures emerge as if by chance, but smart leaders like Walt Freese know that they cannot rely on the Fates alone. Across our interviews there was a broad consensus that, whatever else the CEO is doing, it is absolutely vital for him or her to be engaged in stewarding, shaping, and modeling the culture. As marketing veteran Belinda Lang puts it, "Culture depends on the leadership. They determine the environment that is fostered. The leader sets the tone for the team."

Randy Altschuler is executive chairman of CloudBlue, a company he cofounded to provide recycling services for electronic equipment, including computers, servers, printers, and smartphones. CloudBlue has grown rapidly and now has 16 facilities across the country. Altschuler concurs with Lang's view regarding the critical role of top leadership: "The CEO has to be a model for the whole company, setting the tone and providing an example for others to imitate. Everything about you sends a message— from the size of your office to the hours you work, to the way you treat your subordinates."

Kathryn Hall, CEO and co-chief investment officer at Hall Capital Partners LLC, puts the responsibility for culture on the entire C-suite. "Everybody in senior management must be culture carriers," she says. "It is empty of meaning if you don't walk the walk every day. The CEO, in particular, must be able to identify the values clearly and keep reinforcing them, especially in a people business. Otherwise, other characteristics creep in. You have got to communicate your values often, and publicly." That is how a culture is established.

Physical openness on the part of the CEO counts too. Dolf van den Brink, president and CEO of Heineken USA, thoroughly transformed his old-style national headquarters in White Plains, New York, to reflect his determination to reshape his corporate culture into one that is more open and less hierarchical. He had the old interior torn out and replaced with a free-flowing work area surrounded by offices, their walls made entirely of glass. There was overt symbolism to the remodeling, but it was also meant to create a social ecosystem in which the constituent parts are constantly aware of what all the others are doing.

It is not easy to explain what culture is or how it grows. But it is readily apparent how critical it is to business success. It is something that CEOs need to think about daily. And, as the next chapter will explore, the fostering and maintenance of culture begins right at the beginning of every employee's experience with the company—at the moment of hiring.

QUESTIONS TO ASK YOURSELF

- What are you doing to make your workplace more cohesive, more like a highly functional family unit than a disparate collection of individuals?
- What more could you do to ensure your company operates under a strong and consistently applied set of values? Are you articulating them in a way that everyone understands?
- How well do your corporate values differentiate your company to the outside world?
- How well do the leaders of your organization live the values the company espouses?
- As a member of the C-suite, how high is culture development on your list of daily priorities? What are you doing to strengthen it week by week?

CHAPTER 5

MEASURE TWICE, HIRE ONCE

Cultural fit is both the filter and the continuing framework by which we identify people we want to hire.
— *Kathryn Hall, CEO and chief investment officer,*
Hall Capital Partners

THE GAME OF TALENT BEGINS WITH HIRING. IT IS something forward-minded CEOs think a lot about—*Am I attracting the best people? Am I hiring the right talent for today's needs—and tomorrow's? What can I do to make my company more appealing to the kinds of employees I most want to entice?* These and a hundred related questions feed into this ever-perplexing subject of hiring.

I have found the following five questions to be enormously helpful as I consider candidates. Naturally, they must be bundled with more specific probes related to the person's skills and experiences—if I need someone with expertise in graphic design or art direction or any other specialization, there will be bottom-line requirements that must be met. Beyond those, though, are a handful of additional attributes that make a person especially suited to today's altered workplace. As you sit across the table from potential hires, you might ask yourself,

1. Do they show passion?
2. Will they sync with the team?
3. Would I want to spend time with them?
4. Are they a good cultural fit?
5. Will they meet future needs?

DO THEY SHOW PASSION?

We look for people who are not going to be stopped; they love the work that much.

—*Kris Szafranski, director of*
organizational change, The Nerdery

No matter what business you are in, the right people will show a palpable zest for it and for their potential role in pushing the company's mission forward. Mellody Hobson is president of Ariel Investments, one of America's top minority-owned money management and mutual fund companies; she is also chairman of the board of DreamWorks Animation and a regular guest on ABC's *Good Morning America*. In a conversation with me, she ranked zeal even above skills in those she hires: "I am looking more and more with an eye toward passion and energy and smarts. The skills can be picked up in whatever area you need." She adds, "Warren Buffett asks in job interviews, 'Are you a fanatic?' And I ask that, too. Now some people take it negatively, and that speaks to me. Because in business, I do not think fanaticism is a bad thing." The person who sleeps and breathes having a better customer experience or delivering better service—that is the type she seeks. "I am looking for work ethic, for people who can succeed against adversity. It is not just, 'Are you savvy in digital?'"

The vast majority of senior leaders we surveyed (84 percent) said that, like Hobson, they would hire someone who is smart and passionate even if the person did not yet have the required skills for the position.[1] I feel the same: I remember one hire I made that had much more to do with the person's attitude than his resume. The nature of our industry requires that we stay in constant tune with what's next. To do that, we need to have hard skills in place to deliver to our clients whatever they need in terms of technology, creative services, strategy, and so on. On this occasion, I was looking to fill a senior leadership position for an innovation component within our business. I had interviewed at least ten people with solid credentials. I had little hope for the final person I met with, but his letter had inspired me. In it, he talked about his personal passion for making things easier for people to use. He shared a deeply personal story of an event in his life that triggered this interest and prompted him to pursue a master's degree in anthropology. On paper, he was not a fit. The more I talked with him, though, the more I realized he had a vision for how to create more innovative user experiences. I decided to take the risk and bring him on board. In the end, he was one of the best people I have ever hired, was a star with us, and has gone on to do amazing things in his career.

> **Eighty-four percent of senior business leaders surveyed agree: "I am most interested in hiring people who are smart and passionate, even if they do not yet possess the skills we need."**

WILL THEY SYNC WITH THE TEAM?

Forbes Media chairman and editor in chief Steve Forbes told us that he resolutely declines to hire people who would not be a good fit for his team, even if they are super-talented. Likewise, Mellody Hobson pays particular attention to whether candidates will fit the cultural dynamic and, in particular, mesh with the team. In interviews, she says, "I ask them lots of questions about what drives them, how they measure success, how they think about failure, how they work with others. At Ariel, you cannot be successful if you are a lone wolf. We believe that strong teams lead to better outcomes, and we want diversity of experiences and backgrounds in those teams."

At web-application company 37signals in Chicago, potential employees are taken out for a test drive—given a small project to complete so the rest of the team can assess how well they handle it, including how they communicate with others. In their bestselling book *Getting Real*, company cofounder Jason Fried and partner David Heinemeier Hansson explain, "Working with someone as they design or code a few screens will give you a ton of insight. You'll learn pretty quickly whether or not the right vibe is there. Scheduling can be tough for this sort of thing but even if it's for just 20 or 40 hours, it's better than nothing. If it's a good or bad fit, it will be obvious. And if not, both sides save themselves a lot of trouble and risk by testing out the situation first."[2]

At Havas Worldwide, we often take a similar approach. In our business, a vigorous cottage industry of freelancers exists. Sometimes people freelance between jobs; other times they do it longer term. Whenever possible, I promote a mutual "play period" whereby we can get to know one another prior to making a more serious commitment.

GIVE YOUR TEAM A SAY

With team fit so important, it is hardly surprising that an increasing number of companies are actually letting teams make the hiring decisions in the first place. Cloud-computing firm Rackspace made a recent "toughest places to interview" list.[3] Henry Sauer says that this is thanks in part to its six- to eight-hour interviews chock-full of behavioral questions and conducted by teams. "The whole group debates the candidate, and we have a defined voting process that errs on the side of us *not* making a hire, interestingly enough."

It is a promising approach because who better to determine whether someone is a good fit for the team than the team itself? At DreamWorks, the interview process includes a meet-and-greet with the hiring manager, along with a cross section of other managers and peers. Ten to 15 associates vet most job candidates, whether in person or via video conferencing.[4]

WOULD I WANT TO SPEND TIME WITH THEM?

Your mother was right: It really is important to be a friendly, helpful, personable individual—in short, to be someone with whom others want to spend time. I have heard the same refrain repeatedly from the leaders of companies across the nation: They are looking for employees not only with strong minds and strong skill sets but also with a seemingly effortless ability to communicate—and get along—with others. Dave Lewis, president of the personal care division at Unilever, is one of those leaders: "When I'm meeting with people," he told me, "I spend far more time determining whether their values are in line with the company's. Do they show empathy? Do they care? I look for what they are like as people as much or more than, 'Can they do the task?'"

This focus on the person rather than just the resume makes sense for a whole host of reasons:

- We live in a hyperconnected age of constant engagement—an environment that is more global and diverse than ever before.
- We are laboring in an ideas economy, in which ongoing and multifaceted collaboration is essential.
- We inhabit an era of free-agent talent, a time when the most coveted individuals have nearly unlimited options in terms of where they work.
- Thanks to digital, many of us have hugely expanded the range of folks with whom we interact.

All of these contribute to a scenario in which interpersonal skills matter more than ever.

When I am considering prospective hires, I pore over the materials they have supplied and check them out online, but I also consider the impact they will have on the people who work with them and on the company as a whole. Sometimes it seems to come down to one simple test: *Would I want to have a drink with this person?*

That sounds simplistic, perhaps—but what would be the benefit of bringing on someone who is a brilliant director or strategist if no one wants to spend time with him or her? After all, the workday is an exercise in constant human interaction and interplay. And if I hire someone who pollutes the office environment, might I not eventually lose somebody else who flees from this pest? And why would I want such an individual to represent my company to clients and others?

Henry Sauer takes a similar approach. He maintains that the focus of interviews at Rackspace is not just to check skills and references but also to determine, "is this person human, and do they have a heart for service?" Though the company is eager to find Linux system administrators, a scarce commodity right now, they will reject any candidate who is a poor fit. "We work as teams and expect every Racker to be able to have a conversation with our customers, who are often not IT people. We have got to be translators and to humanize IT."

NO JERKS ALLOWED

If being personable matters so much these days, the corollary holds true as well: There is no room for jerks. Today's equal-opportunity, dressed-down, easygoing workplaces may be models of tolerance in most respects, but not in this one. It is something we heard in our interviews repeatedly. I thought Donna Morris, senior vice president of people resources at Adobe Systems, put it best: She told us their team-centered culture has "antibodies that reject anybody who might be a jerk."

In her conversation with me, marketer Belinda Lang emphasized the need for optimists who raise morale versus "toxic people who undermine the team. The leader's role may need to be to remove them." At Ariel Investments, Mellody Hobson is even more emphatic: "I wouldn't hire someone who does not treat people well. We don't have smart jerks here."

Screening out jerks is a smart policy. No matter how many enticements an organization has to offer, nothing outweighs the negatives of working in a culture where a few backbiting sharks or perpetual grumblers sour the air.

ARE THEY A GOOD CULTURAL FIT?

The previous chapter stressed the immense business value of having a strong culture. But how do you go about maintaining that culture, especially as your company grows? The key ingredient, I believe, is hiring for cultural fit. Leaders who are clear about the culture they want to foster or retain create a self-reinforcing loop by intelligently factoring culture into the hiring process.

In the whole arena of talent, this can be one of the hardest things to achieve. Skills can be readily evaluated and tested; fit is necessarily more qualitative and therefore more subjective (even when you have guiding principles like Arnold Worldwide's vision and values). I made a hire a few years ago who looked great on paper. He came with glowing recommendations. The first six months went really well, but then we started to see another side. He was a "me first" person, but we were trying to build a "we first" culture. In client meetings, he had to be the one who spoke the most, answered all of the questions, and took all of the "air time." While this bothered me, the problem ran deeper than these mere irritants. We are a business that is built by great ideas developed by diverse thinkers— not sole practitioners. It took us a while to figure out what this person was costing our culture and sense of unity, but when we did, we realized he would never be a good long-term fit. He and I had a candid dialogue and decided to part ways. I learned a lesson: It is better to eliminate a poor cultural fit early on rather than risk lasting damage.

I had a similar experience just recently, only this time it was with a company rather than an individual. We tried them out on a small project before committing to a longer-term partnership and, based on that experience, decided that, though they were world class and well known, they simply were not a good fit for us. We were creating a "lean forward" culture—aggressively future focused—and, despite their brilliance, they were far too "lean back," too content to settle for the status quo rather than always stretching toward the next thing. We enjoyed a productive working relationship, but it clearly was not meant to be permanent.

ARE YOUR VALUES ALIGNED?

Every culture is different, and hiring criteria must reflect that. As I indicated earlier, I hire on shared values—on philosophy of life, even, and on agreeing about where our industry is going and what successful agencies need to do to get there.

This syncs with what Mike Bailen, recruiting manager at Zappos, told us about his experience of being a candidate there: "I learned that it is extremely important to consider the company's core values before applying to make sure that they align with your own values. If you firmly believe in a company you are working for and love what you are doing at that company, you will ultimately be more successful."

Bailen notes that every company is currently vying for the best and brightest, particularly in the technology space—but the way Zappos defines the "very best worker" is distinctive in laying heavy emphasis on cultural fit. That fit includes adhering to the company's ten core values, such as "delivering WOW through service," "creating fun and a little weirdness," and "being humble."[5] Not everybody will choose to work for a company that encourages wacky contests and noisy parades through the office. Nor will every upper-level hire be willing to start his or her new job by undergoing a month of training in a variety of departments, including the call center—a requirement at Zappos. In a remarkable practice, every employee must answer phones during the holiday rush, so you might even end up chatting with celebrity CEO Tony Hsieh.[6]

Questions routinely asked during the Zappos interview process include the likes of "On a scale of one to ten, how weird are you?" The answer is deemed less important than the way the applicant reacts. "We are looking for candidates that are a match technically (can they do the job?) and also culturally (do they roll the same way Zappos does?)," says Bailen. "So, in a market that is already saturated by recruiters and head-hunters, we are very particular." They can afford to be particular: Such is its cultural appeal that, in 2012, Zappos expected to receive 30,000 applications for around 600 open slots.

At Grand Circle Travel in Boston, a leading outfit for small-ship and river cruising worldwide, they have set up a group interview system that lays emphasis on values first and skills second on the premise that it is a lot easier to train people to have the right skills than to have the right values. In the hiring process, "it often helps the candidate self-select, so people don't waste our time and theirs," says Denise Sablone, president of worldwide business operations. "We want to be honest with people, letting them know what this culture is like."

At Palo Alto Software in Oregon, chief executive Sabrina Parsons says she definitely would decline to hire somebody who is a poor cultural match:

> *In fact, trying to understand if a person will fit the culture is more of an indicator of future success than anything else. And sometimes we have gotten it wrong. There was a time we hired a person who had this phenomenal background, everything we needed, but he had only worked at large agencies. We have only 40 people; we act like a startup. And he just could not fit. He needed a lot more support. At the old company, he had an assistant; his team had an assistant. They had these long processes. What they did in twelve weeks, we would do it in two. And he couldn't deal with that. I would say to him, "You are in charge, you make the call!" And he couldn't do that. He would say, "Where's the committee, where's the meeting?"*

Parsons goes on to explain,

> *We have no middle management. We have an "expert culture." If we do not know something, we become experts on it ourselves. That is the person who is successful here, the "I'll figure it out" person. But a lot of people are not like that. They want to hear, "This is how it should be done." When somebody says to me, "Give me exactly what you want me to do, and I will do it," it makes me want to pull my hair out. If I was going to give you exactly what I want you to do, why don't I just do it myself?!*

The bottom line is that Parsons has a precise expectation for what the culture should be like at her company. And she is not interested in bringing on board people who will constantly run afoul of it. She always hires to cultural fit.

SCREENING OUT THOSE WHO HAVE DRUNK A COMPETITOR'S KOOL-AID

Clothing retailer American Eagle Outfitters was founded in 1977 and has grown to more than 1,000 stores, 35,000 employees, and $3.2 billion in sales. The company prides itself on a nondictatorial, nonbureaucratic culture that is forgiving and keeps everybody involved. Creativity and innovation are strongly encouraged, with talent at every level free to pitch ideas and be entrepreneurial on their own account.

"We turn a blind eye to some of the moonlighting that is discouraged elsewhere," chief marketing officer Michael Leedy told us. "For example, we have designers on our team who have their own stores, and graphic designers who have web businesses selling their own posters."

American Eagle's hierarchy is flat, and decision making is a nuanced process that involves many people somehow coming to a conclusion. The company is proud of having a culture that is different from those of its rivals, and so it is cautious about hiring people who have worked elsewhere in the industry: "We know our competitors' cultures very well," says Leedy, "and when we interview people from those companies we are hypersensitive to cues that tell us if they will have a hard time breaking out of that mold."

I heard something similar from Henry Sauer. So important is this question of hiring for cultural fit that Rackspace has put into place a "manager detox" for upper-level hires to ensure that outside cultures do not pollute their own. Sauer explains, "The three-day onboarding process is aimed at helping managers to unlearn what they learned at other companies about how to manage people, such as using title as a way to get things done, or coming in with the assumption that what you did elsewhere is going to work here. Instead, you should start by listening and tapping into the knowledge and wisdom of the Rackers who work for you. The job of manager is about *coaching* and *guiding* and *serving* the people that work for you, not being directive and telling them what to do."

WILL THEY MEET FUTURE NEEDS?

A central theme of this book is adaptability: the need for companies to be immensely agile, ready to respond to the fast-changing, even chaotic conditions that are sure to lurk ahead. No wonder companies are now finding that it makes sense to look well into the future, to hire people who have the potential to grow the business regardless of whether there is a current need for their skill set.

Hiring talent without actually having a slot for that person may seem an unusual approach with budgets so tight, but I have done it myself, many times. If I find someone I think will fit the culture and will actively look for ways to push the business forward, I want them on my team. We can figure out the specifics as we go. Because hiring is no longer just about finding the perfect round peg for a round hole or matching an individual to a fully articulated job description. The way I see it, if you are only hiring to fill open positions, your business model is nothing but the status quo.

> **If you are only hiring to fill open positions, your business model is nothing but the status quo.**

At Arnold, we made a number of calculated bets. One of the biggest was bringing on a new chief digital officer, along with 11 other new people. They had left their previous company en masse, and we were building out our digital competency further. We had no accounts to put them on immediately, but we knew that talent like this does not wait around and is extremely hard to find. Their backgrounds were mostly from outside our industry—from client-side technology companies, software companies, and tech startups. We knew that this wasn't where our business was today, but it most certainly was where it was headed. After intense discussions, including hours on the phone every day for ten days, we decided to go ahead. In the end, this bet paid off. Today, they are all fully baked into the business and helping in vital ways to modernize the company and clients' marketing. The new skill set they brought enabled us to expand the work we did for current clients and was pivotal to winning new clients. For example, in a pitch for a major global financial services company, members of the new team helped us to conceive and develop an inspiring vision for the future of online banking and mobile commerce. This thinking not only secured us the digital component of the relationship but also was pivotal to our winning the whole assignment.

Clearly, you cannot hire this way without a solid strategic plan behind you. But I firmly believe you need to place strategic bets and then do what you have to in order to garner the talent that will make those bets pay off.

Hiring is never easy, but doing it in a smart way, as in the examples cited earlier, forms the essential first step in building a truly talent-centric company. It is critical to laying the foundations of a versatile and agile workforce that will serve you well both today and tomorrow.

QUESTIONS TO ASK YOURSELF

- What more can you do to try out candidates with the team before you add them to your roster?
- Are you hiring with an eye to the future rather than simply to fill current openings? What practices would assist you in identifying future needs?
- Do you have adequate measures in place to vet whether a candidate will contribute to or detract from the cohesive environment you have tried to build?
- How can you better measure for raw ability, brains, passion, and potential during the hiring process rather than simply focusing on the candidate's existing skills?

STRATEGY TWO

DON'T MANAGE . . . LEAD!

Executives don't deliver the goods. They only steer the ship.
—Alexis Nasard, chief commercial
officer, Heineken N.V.

CHAPTER 6

EQUIP YOUR PLAYERS

THE SEEDS ARE BEING SOWN TODAY FOR A VERY different type of company, culture, and employee. Rather than closely monitored and hierarchical environments in which conflicting interests are pitted against each other and compromises reached, workplaces are becoming more collective and holistic—highly interdependent networks in which everybody's interests are woven together.

Pivotal to the new way of doing business are two factors that were in short supply in the businesses of old: trust (the antithesis of the traditional command-and-control culture) and empowerment. Rather than follow orders, workers are given clear information so that they are able to make intelligent decisions on their own.

How do you get your company aligned with these new values? My advice: Spend less time managing and more time doing. We try hard to follow this dictum at Havas Worldwide. While we still consider it critical for a company of our size and complexity to employ people with traditional management titles, we believe the time they spend managing should be minimized and the time they spend actively participating in activities maximized. In our most successful companies, almost without exception, the management—especially the senior management—are actively engaged in our craft and doing hands-on work for our client businesses. That means our most senior people are deeply involved in everything from brainstorming ideas to pitching accounts and developing creative for our clients. They don't clock out at the close of the official business day as their teams struggle to meet tight deadlines, and their job isn't just to give the thumbs up or down to the work their teams produce. They are players on their teams, not simply coaches or managers.

At the same time that we are creating an environment in which managers spend the bulk of their time "doing" rather than managing, we are working at the other end to ensure all team players—at whatever level—have the tools and trust they need to succeed without anyone hovering over their shoulders. To be effective, this requires a shared understanding of our agency goals and the specific objectives of each particular client project. In the absence of such an understanding, it would be impossible for team members to work without direct—and near constant—supervision.

How do you create a workplace centered more on a shared vision than on rules? A few basic principles will help:

- Let the information cascade down.
- Empower the team.
- Get down in the trenches.

We'll look at these concepts one by one.

LET THE INFORMATION CASCADE DOWN

Vital to empowering employees is giving them plenty of information about what is going on. As CEO, it is all too easy to surround yourself with your direct reports and neglect to share information and insights with people further down the chain. Starting at Arnold and now continuing at Havas Worldwide, I have regularly brought our younger staff together for what we call Breakfast Banter with Benett—time set aside for me to share our vision, listen to ideas and concerns, and answer questions. There is no set agenda. I spend an hour and a half once a month with a group composed of our younger top-performing people—selected by their managers. They share, and I share. In the end, the topics discussed matter less than the fact that a meaningful dialogue is taking place. I always encourage them to leave the lines of communication wide open—and many do.

The dialogue at these breakfasts typically starts slowly. To get things going, I usually talk about how and why I entered the industry and why I came to our particular company. We then share our perspectives on what is working and what is not (even if that includes me). One of the things I learned after a few of these sessions was that there was a real need for more dialogue and knowledge sharing around what the global network is up to. It shocked me how little people knew. I had thought we were doing a good job of communicating; as it turns out, we not only were failing to communicate "out" enough, we also were not doing a very good job of listening "in." This realization informed our internal communications plans, and we had a small group help us with key aspects of our intranet— a new central hub for information gathering and sharing.

Meeting in person with up-and-coming contributors to your organi- zation may seem like an obvious thing to do, but obvious things too often are overlooked by busy professionals, even though they can make a tre- mendous difference. A small example from my experience: Early in my consulting career, I was working hard on a strategic recommendation for the repositioning of a major division of a technology company that was on the brink of extinction. I knew what my deliverable was, but I was not clued in to the totality of what we were doing, its full magnitude and potential import. That changed the moment I sat down to review my thinking with the partner in charge; he spent time explaining how my work fit into the larger scheme of reorganizing the marketing department of our client and how, in doing so, we were changing how the company would in turn interact with its customers. This context helped make my thinking better and also gave me an even greater sense of purpose: I wasn't only helping to reengineer a department, I was actually helping to save a company. Afterward, this partner thoughtfully asked me to describe what I was enjoying and not enjoying about the assignment. It took him just an hour, but I have never forgotten how helpful it was to me and my professional development at that early stage in my career.

In the world of business, it is dismaying how often even the most fundamental information is not shared. According to a broad 2011 survey of U.S. employees, only half of bosses involve their employees actively in decision making, and when decisions are made, only 43 percent bother to explain the thinking that lies behind those decisions.[1] Instead of healthy transparency, this reveals a widespread culture of murky opaqueness. Workers are deliberately being left in the dark.

Not so at the most inspiring, talent-forward places. "We put heavy emphasis on daily check-ins or standups with the team," so everybody has copious information about what is up, says The Nerdery's Kris Szafranski. "Every two to four weeks, everyone gets individual attention. We let managers know that this expectation exists. We put a significant amount of time into 'face time' . . . but it has been well worth it."

At his previous jobs, Szafranski did not have this kind of face time unless he actively sought it out. "It was hands-off, and managers did not seek out dialogue. I did not get it then why open communication is so vital—but now I think it is important, and I have kept it as a key part of this organization. It gives employees insight into what goes on outside of their day-to-day. It demystifies the management layer; otherwise, you cannot see above the layer of your manager. You can ask questions and voice ideas. It becomes a more fulfilling place to be, and we see that in people's output. Plus, employees tend to collaborate more."

As information flows freely, every level is empowered. "We encourage all employees to voice ideas and solve problems," Szafranski says. "We have several departments and roles that only exist because people saw a need and got the support to fill it. Those areas are now keys to our success."

"Too often talent is viewed as commodities," says Walt Freese. He has seen the value in involving everyone in the company's inner workings: "It can't be just me," he says about driving change and progress at the company. "The key so often to effective leadership is, you need to help to lead people to their own insights. Then they fully embrace it. Otherwise, it is simply the CEO's idea."

His advice is to "give people information and space to form their own insights. It cannot be manufactured; it has to be authentic." He urges a constant flow of facts and opinions stemming from "a desire to engage employees in dialogue. Let them know their thoughts and opinions are truly valued. This requires a culture where it is safe to offer any idea, challenge any strategy, ask any question. Over time they will come to believe that 'This is our company, this is our mission.'"

Giving everyone a voice empowers every level of the organization. When a single, hourly worker's idea is adopted, the ripple effect can be powerful: "For a line worker, seeing one of his or her peers having an effect on the company is incredibly impactful." The benefits of soliciting fresh thoughts are numerous, Freese adds: "If employees have an opportunity to be heard, even if the company doesn't use their idea, they have far more buy-in."

GET THE CONVERSATION ROLLING

Starting and engaging in conversations is essential to good leadership and is also a smart way to help steer the conversation. We all know that talk is going to happen, even in companies that do their best to stifle the flow of information. All too often, this talk is full of grumbles and gripes, innuendo and misinformation. To be sure the right information is being released in a timely manner, "you need to constantly be listening to the chatter in the group," says Bob O'Leary, head of global marketing for the consumer business at Citi. "You have got to have a pulse on what is going on." Companies with the freest exchange of information, aboveboard and constant, suffer least from toxic, behind-the-scenes grousing.

O'Leary speaks from experience, having helped turn around the culture at Citi after the financial collapse of 2009: "We worked hard to improve talent and morale," he says and in a way, that was far more democratic than previously was typical for the company. Through a new Voice of the Employee survey, input was sought from everybody, with the goal of "understanding what motivates people and addressing their needs in a very transparent way." What were they grumbling about back then? "A lack of clear roles and responsibilities," says O'Leary. "A lack of communication and transparency. Lack of payment-for-performance perceptions. Not enough learning opportunities. Too many obstacles in the way of being successful. We were coming out of that dark period."

Armed now with critical information, O'Leary could make decisive changes. "We created an action plan around engagement, meritocracy, and process. We went through and said, 'You told us this, we did that.' People started to realize we were creating a culture where their morale and happiness were being addressed." The lesson he learned is that talent is absolutely critical but time consuming. "We work on it every week. It requires a ton of attention. You cannot do it with a fraction of your time. But it is vital. Talent is the number one asset we have. If you don't pay attention to it, it dies on the vine."

At Care.com, founder and chief executive Sheila Marcelo is vigilantly alert to water-cooler buzz. Far from ignoring it, she addresses it with bold directness in organization-wide meetings. "For example," she says, "we hired a couple of vice presidents, and the rumor mill got going about 'Why are we hiring senior people?' So I mentioned this in the meeting. And I said, 'It sounds like there are issues, so let's walk through why we are doing this.' I showed them the 2013 strategy on the projector and went through the game plan, and everyone was nodding, 'Yes!'"

Marcelo is passionate about keeping lines of communication wide open. "There are two major products we have launched lately," she says. "And some people are asking, 'Did everything just blow up in our day job?' So I need to walk people through the vision. Too often, executives assume people will just go with the flow, like they are robots."

INFORMATION FLOW IS CRITICAL FOR DISTRIBUTED DECISION MAKING

A freer flow of facts is especially urgent now that decision making is of necessity more distributed. Justin Menkes, author of *Better Under Pressure* and a consultant with executive search firm Spencer Stuart, cites the digital explosion as a reason that information—and decision making—now must be pushed down lower and lower into the organization: There simply is no way senior executives can handle it all on their own. "The people you are managing are so global, and there is so much data your direct reports have that you do not have," Menkes explains. "So you have got to delegate. You have no choice but to be more dependent now on your people and their expertise." Today's CEO must think, vis-à-vis his or her employees, "'You know your job better than I do.' CEOs have a global role and must be external-facing—so they are highly dependent on their teams."

Wherever they sit within the organization, talented people working on complex issues oftentimes know more about the topic than decision makers higher up—and they know they do. Speaking about his time as vice president of product engineering at Netflix, John Ciancutti told me he made it a point to organize things so that the people with the information were actually charged with making the vital choices: "I found that my team was in a better position to make decisions than I was because they were immersed in it all day. My job was shallower and broader, and my boss's was shallower and broader than that. My role was to build an outstanding team. I held them accountable for their decisions."

Michael Zea, a former McKinsey partner and current president and CEO of loyalty management company Aimia's U.S. region, says he actively seeks out people who are proactive and will take ownership of decisions. "Some colleagues ask me, 'What's the plan?' and I reply to them, 'What's *your* plan?' Their perspectives are important, and I want to hear what they have to say. Otherwise, you're not going to get the best solution, and people are going to tune out because you are just telling them what to do and, in my experience, that does not work—especially with younger generations."

EMPOWER THE TEAM

As a top executive, you are not just overseeing scattered individuals. You are responsible for organizing them into effective teams—the sum totals of which are greater than their parts—by the magic alchemy of good team building. Early in my career, when I was running the brand-strategy practice for consultancy FutureBrand, I first clued in to something important: The tight, well-knit team that enjoys working together can tremendously outperform any group—no matter how talented—that is less tightly bound.

In consulting, the assignments are generally short term and extremely intense. We always assembled well-integrated, diverse teams, but some teams did better than others. One day I brought this up at our management meeting. We discussed it and debated why certain teams outperformed others and then reconvened a few days later after we had gathered more data. Ultimately, we concluded that our highest-performing team liked each other the most. They broke for dinners. They went bowling. They cared about one another. Cohesion led to performance that far outstripped any other team we had.

Team making is a subtle art, but it is one that all of us in the C-suite have got to master—for teams are the talent wave of tomorrow. At Rackspace, all employees take the Gallup StrengthsFinder aptitude test, and their top five strengths are posted on their desks and even stamped on their security badges.[2] That makes it easy for teams of people with complementary skills to be assembled swiftly, but I think it also serves as an elegant reminder that the company is made up of a diverse group of people who are strongest when their aptitudes are combined.

Ford Motor Company has lately undertaken a cultural transformation under the rubric, "One team, one plan, one Ford." It began with new CEO Alan Mulally, who was dismayed by the many silos he found. According to Felicia J. Fields, group vice president, human resources and corporate services, Mulally said, "'We have to come together as one team'—and that was the beginning of culture change." She adds, "The configuration of teams, of virtual teams, is exploding. So many people work with people they never see. How do you govern those teams? And across multiple time zones? It really tests your ability, when the team is not in the same workspace."

Ford's HR department now offers classes on building high-performing teams. They do diagnostic tests and emphasize soft skills and team dynamics: "We help them set their strategies, look at their own strategic priorities, how to hold themselves accountable." Under the "one Ford" banner, they have successfully created a single team model, Fields explains. In the past, "I would have had 25 different models" in various regions of the world. "Now, we have one common process for developing our teams."

THE MIDDLE IS YOUR CORE

Team-centric management helps the middle level of the organization become far more productive and more apt to churn out good ideas, says Mike Abbott of Kleiner Perkins Caufield & Byers. He sees a strong trend toward empowering the middle levels of companies. "Historically, it was very top down on the 'what.' Now the 'what' is emerging from the crowd, from the employees. And you get better ideas. People are realizing that the best ideas come from the team, not from an executive. And executives are getting more comfortable with 'what they don't know.' You have to be like this to be competitive today. Every employee wants to make an impact."

Companies must present themselves as places where people in the middle tiers can have a powerful impact, or the most talented people will not come work for you. Abbott knows what he is talking about: He is famous for having grown Twitter's engineering team from 80 engineers to more than 350 in less than a year and a half, scaling Twitter's architecture to support 250 million daily tweets.

Recently, I asked everybody in our organization how we could all collaborate more effectively and achieve greater diversity of thought. Someone shared the idea of having Havas Lofts in ten of our key markets—residences where people could stay for two weeks at a time in order to work on a particular assignment in a different country. It seems like an excellent idea, not expensive, and likely to prove a win for both company and employee—so it is now in the works.

GET DOWN IN THE TRENCHES

Everyone is watching the top brass: Are they in the trenches with the foot soldiers or studying lines on the map from some cushy headquarters far from the front? If I have learned anything, it is that the days of the aloof CEO peering down from Olympian heights are over. You have to jump into the muddy fray with everybody else.

Randy Altschuler of CloudBlue put it well:

> As CEO, you have got to be down on the floor. Remember the old Star Trek episodes—where the Enterprise had hundreds of crew, presumably, but you always saw Captain Kirk and Spock and Bones out there risking their lives on every mission? As a kid I wondered, "Why not send your subordinates sometimes?" But when you start a company, you realize you have got to be on the front lines. I hate the plant manager sitting in his office; when I see a person spending most of his day in his office, I know it is not going to work out. Open floor plans—they really work. There should not be any closed-door stuff. There should not be any secrets.

Many leaders need to jettison their grandiose self-images. "A leader serves," says Stewart McHie, who runs the master's degree program in business analysis at Catholic University and spent 34 years at ExxonMobil. "Leadership is about setting the vision—but also about serving employees and customers. Ego and personality are marketable; they get you on TV. But true leadership is not about chest thumping and trying to become a celebrity. That is just self-aggrandizement." Justin Menkes agrees: "The best CEOs," he says, "spend a tremendous amount of time with their people, making sure they understand their roles. It is not *directive* anymore, but being a *servant*: 'How can I help you?' You must own the strategy, must lay out the vision, and after that it becomes an exercise of being a servant."

Now it may be scary for some members of the C-suite to discard the armor of ego and authority, but it has to be done. At the National Cable & Telecommunications Association, president and chief executive

Michael K. Powell stresses the importance to business of fostering a climate in which employees can criticize everything they find amiss—including you. He admires how airlines teach copilots how to speak up and criticize their pilots, who, after all, are only human. To foster this atmosphere of ready criticism, Powell says, "The leadership needs to have sufficient self-confidence and be comfortable in their own skin. It requires humility: 'My paycheck may be bigger than yours . . . but I could still be wrong!'"

Powell makes it a point to surround himself with the opposite of yes-men. "I am a big believer in kitchen cabinets. People to whom I can say, 'Here are my doubts. Am I doing this right?' 'I am anxious about this—should I be doing it?' If I do not have people like that, I hire them. I need someone to beat me around a little."

The best leaders understand that no task lies "beneath their pay grade." At Care.com, Sheila Marcelo recently spent two hours meeting with the stalwarts of the Fun Force committee—the social activities chairs. They were unhappy about something or other, and Marcelo needed to find out what. "And HR said to me, 'You do not have a couple of hours to spend on this.' But I said to them, 'They are the social club, and if *they* aren't having fun. . . .'" What she saw was that the larger morale was at stake—maybe even the cultural health of the company.

Why didn't she just let HR handle the problem? "HR is available, but sometimes, by just listening and spending time with employees, they will understand that this is important to me. Sometimes executives focus on 'being the C-suite,' being distant, unapproachable; it is hard to grab them. That creates fear and distance, and it reduces transparency. And that may mean you don't see problems until it becomes too late and they have grown too big to solve easily."

VALVE CORPORATION: TAKING SELF-MANAGEMENT TO EXTREMES

Fans of flat hierarchies and an end to micromanagement will be hard-pressed to find a better example than Valve Corporation, a video-game company based in Washington State. Valve has no managers, no chain of command. It says so plain and clear in its employee handbook, on page 4: "Valve is flat. It's our shorthand way of saying that we don't have any management, and nobody 'reports to' anybody else. We do have a founder/president, but even he isn't your manager."[3]

In practical terms, this means employees decide for themselves how they will spend their time. They choose which projects they want to work on and physically move to join the project. That puts a lot of responsibility on each person, but as the handbook says, "You were not hired to fill a specific job description. You were hired to constantly be looking around for the most valuable work you could be doing."[4]

Valve takes countercultural, nobody-in-charge idealism to quite an extreme, but it seems to work. It is a private company, so precise financials are not known, but it is valued at $4 billion and is said to have 400 employees and a startling 55 million customers using its Steam platform. It is believed to achieve higher profitability per employee than Google, Amazon, and Microsoft, and it determines compensation according to co-worker evaluations.[5]

Valve's approach may strike you as either a first step toward corporate anarchy or a smart confederation of entrepreneurs. Either way, it is a trailblazing approach to thinking about talent and, I believe, a rough indication of the direction in which more organizations will be moving—even if not quite to that extreme.

QUESTIONS TO ASK YOURSELF

- What have you done to advance your organization into one that embraces a less controlling, more collective approach?
- What needs to happen to get managers out of their offices and onto the floor?
- What is the conversational tone within your organization? Is it primarily a constructive discussion among well-informed people or murmured asides that muddy the truth and harm cohesion?

- What can be done to boost the level of honest feedback within your organization? How can you make everybody understand it is safe to air their views, even when they conflict with your own?
- What more can you do to make talent feel empowered to add value on their own rather than standing around waiting for instructions?

CHAPTER 7

TRUST THEM

THE NEW TALENT MODEL IS BASED IN LARGE PART ON A fundamental premise: You need to trust your employees to do the job you hired them to do. In fact, the more you trust them, the more value they will provide because they will have room to expand along the lines of their natural abilities and because they generally will be happier on the job.

The best managers have learned the trick of ceding control and seeding trust. When Frank Biondi joined Coca-Cola in 1985, he was astonished by how the company operated, using a method that was then highly innovative: "Coke ran the business by getting great people, giving them great instructions and the tools to do it right, and setting them loose." Biondi described to me how he "grew up in a top-down management structure. At HBO [which he had run previously], I could make every important decision because it wasn't that complex a business, and I could manage it from the top down." When he went to work for Coca-Cola Television, however, he was amazed to see that "they didn't manage the business in Australia or South Africa; they gave them a good game plan and hired good people to execute the plan. It gave me a totally different view." His way of running companies was forever changed by this exposure.

> **What Is a Great Workplace?**
> "Trust is the defining principle…created through management's credibility, the respect with which employees feel they are treated, and the extent to which employees expect to be treated fairly."[1]
> —Great Place to Work Institute

This notion of empowering workers through trust has spread widely. In our own survey, 94 percent of senior executives said the most successful companies trust their employees, giving them the freedom and independence they need to do their jobs well.[2] You can hear this attitude echoed in companies large and small—including at Rackspace, where Henry Sauer told me, "There aren't a lot of policies here. 'Wear clothes to work'—that is the dress code. We take our work for our customers very seriously, but we don't take ourselves too seriously as individuals."

At The Motley Fool, the culture of trust derives directly from Tom and David Gardner, who founded the firm some 20 years ago. The easygoing English majors named the company for the fool in Shakespeare's *As You Like It*, who alone could tell the duke the truth without being punished. Recruiting director Anessa Fike told us about the Gardners: "They trust that adults can be adults, and we do not have to keep watching over you. It is a culture based on trust."

> Ninety-four percent of senior business leaders surveyed agree: "The most successful companies trust their employees, giving them freedom to make decisions and to act with a measure of independence."

WHY TRUST PAYS OFF

Smart companies are instilling cultures and processes based on trust because it:

- Builds unity
- Enhances recruiting

- Optimizes millennials
- Frees you from minutiae

TRUST BUILDS UNITY

Why does a trusting environment produce such satisfied—and pro-ductive—employees? Perhaps it is because they feel like part of a high-functioning family instead of cogs in an industrial wheel, their every motion sternly and skeptically eyed from above. Google's Larry Page was recently asked, "How important to you are Google's wonderful lifestyle perks, from the free food to the massages, for the employee experience you're trying to design?" He replied, "I don't think it's any of those indi-vidual things. It's important that the company be a family, that people feel that they're part of the company, and that the company is like a family to them. When you treat people that way, you get better productivity."[3]

When heightened trust is accorded to each individual, teams get closer. People drive the organization's direction, not some manual of rigid rules. The advantages of this approach are myriad and often unexpected. "The part that many people don't understand is that trust = speed," Sam Cicotello, chief rabble-rouser of the highest order at The Motley Fool, has said in explaining her company's distinctive approach. "Professional trust is very closely related to productivity and output. Trust in the workplace leads to faster decisions, higher collaboration, and greater autonomy. In a high-trust relationship, you focus on the future, and everything moves faster. You can say the wrong thing and still be understood. You can make a mistake and recover quickly—and your team will help you."[4]

TRUST ENHANCES RECRUITING

"There is a business purpose behind this culture of trust," Cicotello adds. "Obviously it makes our Fools happy, improves recruiting, and leads to great employee retention and a healthy office environment. I hope that's pretty obvious."[5] The recruiting part is especially important nowadays, when the most talented workers have so many options. John Lettow has thought a great deal about how empowering the individual employee can bolster recruiting and improve profitability. He cofounded Vorbeck Materials to commercialize a hugely promising substance called graphene, which he calls "the strongest material that has yet been measured." It is a sheet of carbon only one atom thick. Vorbeck uses it as a coating in the printing of electronic circuits. "We can print them on paper, and you can crush it in your hand or throw it in the washing machine," Lettow explains. And graphene can be used in wearable electronics: Instead of strapping on a heart-rate monitor, the monitor will *be* your shirt, and it can talk to your smartphone. Or a high school athlete's football jersey can gauge whether he is getting dehydrated.

To make any of this happen, Lettow needs to build an effective company first. To retain the highest levels of talent, he says, "We try to give people enough independence within the projects to have a significant say about the directions of their projects. We tell people, 'You will be given enough opportunity, and you will be able to take full advantage of your talents and skills. You will not be locked into a track. There will not be hurdles in order for you to have a meaningful role here. This is a true opportunity to show what your talent can yield.'" So Lettow strongly endorses the idea that trust is a new business fundamental. He then gives an example of how Vorbeck trusted a new employee, giving her a substantial degree of responsibility early on: "We had a person who did two internships here; we made an offer to her. Then we brought her into a meeting with a major customer so she could assist and push the project along. We found she was getting a lot of the project done and could communicate its potential very efficiently. Now she runs that account entirely, and she is building a business line around it, a whole product area."

TRUST OPTIMIZES MILLENNIALS

Trust may be of particular relevance to millennials. Baby boomers famously rebelled against their elders ("Don't trust anyone over 30") and strong-armed their way to influence through protest and confrontation. Millennials favor a gentler approach: Their relationship with older generations tends to be close and collaborative.

We have all read media reports of helicopter parents—those over-involved in every detail of their children's lives—but this is a two-way phenomenon. On the job, millennials expect to be on a common footing with the people in charge. After all, they have been unusually close to their parents. A mere 9 percent have ever had a serious disagreement with Mom or Dad, a survey showed, compared with one in five among people over age 30.[6] They expect to be trusted and to feel part of a collaborative effort.

"We found that young employees want to be integrated early into decisions and feel like they have the full picture," says Jim Davey, vice president of global marketing at Timberland. "In the old days, you just did what the boss told you and tried to pick up context where you could, but that's an outdated model. Now you'll often be asked, 'Why am I doing this? What's the bigger picture?'" This can be hard for some bosses who grew up in the traditional, hierarchical model and aren't used to constantly communicating, Davey says.

Havas Creative Group's Matt Howell says his younger colleagues are fully worthy of trust: "I put 25-year-olds in front of chief marketing officers from multibillion-dollar companies, and they are incredibly persuasive. I think clients are smart enough to realize that this is not a stupid oversight, but rather, we are showcasing somebody of real ability. They are seen very creditably by very senior people."

TRUST FREES YOU FROM MINUTIAE

Another advantage of the high-trust approach is that it frees up your executives to pay attention to what really matters for business success—instead of wasting time on minutiae related to what each employee is doing every minute of the day. As Sabrina Parsons of Palo Alto Software put it: "My management style does not lend itself to babysitting people. It is a huge amount of effort to track people: 'When did you go to lunch? When did you come back from lunch?' In today's fast-paced environment, there is no time for me to do that. And is it worth my paying an assistant to do it, to take attendance?"

SO WHAT STANDS IN THE WAY?

If trust yields so many solid benefits, why aren't more CEOs catching on? Unfortunately, in many businesses, harsh economic constraints have convinced management that they should give remorseless scrutiny to what employees do on company time. They micromanage their working hours, eliminate distractions (e.g., banning social media at work), and force employees to fill in detailed time sheets—a modern variation on the old scientific management principles (a.k.a. time and motion) devised by Frederick Taylor a century ago.

Taylor's approach made sense as a way to maximize productivity in the steel industry (its original purpose) and other jobs involving repetitive tasks. But today, it has lost its relevance in most of those businesses that do not need to track billable hours. Even in the best of circumstances, the old controlling approach only works where there are well-defined processes of value creation and little scope for employees to think up new ways of creating value on their own. It is a great system for automatons, not free thinkers.

But time and motion is proving hard to get rid of. After a hundred years, its stern ethos continues to permeate American business. We have all seen its soul-deadening effects. Technology journalist Robert X. Cringely summarizes the kind of corporate mindset that remains all too common: "They want to know what you are doing and when you are doing it. Oh, by the way, without knowing your name."

Nothing tramples the delicate blossom of trust faster than the boot of the micromanager. When Mondelēz recently split from Kraft, the top 400 people in the developing markets division gathered in Istanbul for a week, a kind of founding convention called "Let the Joy Begin." Much of what they talked about pertained to the new company's seven values, including collaboration: "Employees collaborating is a critical part of us trusting each other," Carlos Abrams-Rivera told me. The meeting was basically about, "How do we make certain we understand what our strategies are and how we are going to live our values; not just us talking about financial goals, but what are we going to do differently going forward? How will we operationalize those values?" The 40 top people out of the 400 each led a small-group discussion centered on, "Given these values, what are three things we want to do differently going forward?"

Now what is particularly telling is that one of the most urgent proposals that emerged from all this brainstorming was this: Managers should not automatically tinker with and add to the ideas that their subordinates come up with. Instead, they should show they trust subordinates by letting them develop and implement the ideas on their own. Here was a heartfelt plea for trust instead of micromanagement and oppressive layering.

"If we hire all these great people, we must be sure we can trust them; but the tendency in management is to add to a proposal," Abrams-Rivera explains. So the better approach is, "Maybe there is nothing we need to add to that" instead of "management always adding value." For Abrams-Rivera, the ultimate conclusion is, "Be aware of the signals you send. For managers, how do you manifest that trust? If we are talking about trust, we are living it."

TRUST IN ACTION

In my conversations with top executives, several issues consistently emerged in which trust plays a central role. One is vacation time for employees. I found that the most talent-forward companies have loosened their vacation policies to an extraordinary degree. Speaking about his time at Netflix, John Ciancutti told me, "There is no vacation policy. The company does not track it. I managed about 100 people, and I could not have told you anyone's vacation days, how many they had taken. The policy simply was, 'Take vacation.'" You heard right: According to the company, no mechanism exists whatsoever to track vacation time. Workers decide how much leave to take and when to take it. (There are certain limits: Being out sick for more than five days requires a doctor's note, and time off beyond 30 days annually must be approved by HR.)

Vacation is treated liberally at The Motley Fool, too. "We don't have an HR department that keeps track of vacation and sick days," Anessa Fike says. "We hire hard workers because we know they won't take advantage of that." In fact, workers take less vacation than elsewhere "because they know it is always there." The company tells new hires, "Unlimited vacation? Yes. We trust you to manage your workflow and cover your projects. We also trust that you will manage your time off in a way that makes you happy and doesn't disadvantage your team."[7]

Another arena in which trust comes constantly into play is expensing costs for travel and entertainment. "Act in Netflix's best interests" is the entire policy at that innovative company. And then there is media use. At The Motley Fool, they have an open work environment where it quickly becomes apparent if anybody is abusing social media privileges. Fike told me, "If somebody's on Facebook all day, their teammates can see them." But in fact, "We don't have a problem with it" if an employee uses the web. "It's OK to shop online for an hour as long as you are getting your work done."

When it comes to communicating via social media, the most innovative companies exhibit a refreshing level of trust in their employees. They not only permit their talent to discuss the company via social networks and blogs but actively encourage it. A recent article about Big Blue stresses this approach: "At IBM, it's about losing control. 'We don't have a corporate blog or a corporate Twitter ID because we want the "IBMers" in aggregate to be the corporate blog and the corporate Twitter ID,' says Adam Christensen of social media communications.…Thousands of IBMers are the voice of the company."[8]

THE ADVANTAGES OF OWNERSHIP

If you really want to communicate trust, you should constantly be looking for ways to instill in your talent a feeling both that they belong to the company and that the company belongs to them.

I think they have the right idea at online marketing and web analytics company LivePerson. Founder and CEO Robert LoCascio brought the whole company together to brainstorm about its values statement and ended up making ownership a core value. As he told the *New York Times*: "We eventually got to two core values: be an owner and help others. Be an owner is about us being owners as individuals, driving the business. . . . And what was interesting is when we would be in meetings, somebody would say, 'You're not allowing me to be an owner.' Or I had an employee who came to me and said: 'I'm leaving the company because I don't want this. I can't handle being an owner. I just want to be told what to do.'"

Giving employees a sense of ownership has led directly to innovation, LoCascio says. Workers who would not necessarily have been expected to come up with new products but who were close to the customers and could see what was needed have taken it upon themselves to create innovative solutions. LivePerson has funded these business plans and brought the products to market, with financial compensation paid to the internal entrepreneurs. "We've gone from a one-product company to a five-product company in under a year, and now 15 percent of our bookings are from new products," LoCascio says.[9]

A vigorous sense of ownership goes hand in hand with the entrepreneurial spirit so many companies are trying to kindle. Serial entrepreneur Sev Onyshkevych has seen up close what passionate employee ownership can do for a startup. In 2001, he was running EZsize.com, which offered 3-D body scanning, allowing customers to more reliably buy clothes online. Then came the dot-com bust. Onyshkevych recalls, "We went from $84-million-to-go-global, 'body scanners in every mall,' to that money all having disappeared. We could have just walked away, but we had a great team. People kept coming back to work. They had equity, but they were not getting paid anything. All but one of the 28 came back the next day—and we did get sold, and many got hired by that company. But it was very much an outside chance. In terms of risk versus reward, everybody should have just left the office. You want to have troops like that."

QUESTIONS TO ASK YOURSELF

- How are you showing your trust in your employees and encouraging them to work autonomously?
- What more can you do to give your talent a sense of ownership over the company and its future?
- How might your organization benefit from an internal compensation program for entrepreneurs?

STRATEGY THREE

LIVE WHAT'S NEXT

CHAPTER 8

BE RELENTLESSLY ADAPTIVE

REGARDLESS OF WHAT INDUSTRY YOU ARE IN, YOU KNOW the pace of change is accelerating, and organizations that fail to keep up are fast dropping by the wayside. Hollywood Video, Borders Group, and K•B Toys are just a few of the well-known brands that foundered and ultimately sank in the new economy. The lesson we all have learned is that, even more so than in previous eras, businesses need to respond quickly to changing circumstances in a competitive landscape wildly in flux. The most successful brands will be those like Nike, which, rather than cling to a narrow category, has expanded into the digital world with products such as Nike+ Kinect and FuelBand. Nike has never thought of itself as a footwear or even a sports apparel company; it considers itself a general inspiration and supporter of the athlete within all of us, and that more broadly defined mission gives it plenty of scope to grow.

We all need to reshape our workforces to be relentlessly adaptive—and I am convinced that the best way to accomplish that is to fully empower the individual employee to act in the company's best interests. We all need to free our talent to innovate on their own, to become entrepreneurs. Or as DreamWorks' head of HR, Dan Satterthwaite, put it in an interview, to be their "own CEOs."[1]

Few industries have felt the earthquakes of transformation more than publishing. Steve Forbes, chairman and editor in chief of Forbes Media—and formerly a contender for the U.S. presidency—marvels at how much the industry has changed: "Today, you have to know how to bring diverse people on board and keep track of them. In the past, we printed 1,300 articles in the magazine every year. Now, we have almost 1,000 contributors and publish 120,000 submissions a year on the website. Web traffic is over 45 million unique visitors a month."

The role of the writer is different today too—untethered from the company and the newsroom. "Today's writers don't just write; now they are expected to edit their own copy and to do the promotion for their pieces. They are paid by the traffic they generate personally." The bottom line: "Talent is more diverse than 20 years ago. More and more, they must master all."

In the publishing industry, Forbes makes clear, executives and employees alike have had no choice: They must embrace the new strategy of being adaptive. "Having the ability to see around the corner is more important than ever before," he told me. But what about folks who do not display these modern abilities? "Most of the people who could not readjust have gone. They realized this was no longer the place for them. But that's putting a rather negative spin on things. In fact, there are lots of people who are thriving in this new environment who might not have thrived under the old regime."

What publishing has experienced in the past decade—convulsive, cataclysmic change—is a foretaste of what every kind of business can soon expect to undergo, if it has not already. Forbes points to the wreckage of once-proud companies that are now—as far as print operations go at least—pretty much extinct, including *U.S. News & World Report* and *Newsweek*, both founded in 1933 and seemingly timeless national institutions. Who, even a decade ago, would have anticipated their demise as hold-in-your-hand publications? But Forbes has become accustomed to modern realities, and his company is thriving by embracing change. "If you don't figure it out," he cautions, "you perish."

WHAT'S WRONG AT MEGACORP?

Many companies are facing the kind of looming extinction that Steve Forbes describes because they are not keeping up. They are gravely threatened by their own sluggishness, their hidebound inability to respond quickly, to generate new ideas. Some people go so far as to predict doom, eventually, for every really big company, so great are the dangers of not innovating and so difficult do such companies find it to keep up with their smaller, more agile rivals. Size is proving a serious disadvantage nowadays, and businesses need to be alert to this.

I spoke with John Ciancutti, director of engineering at Facebook, who said that even the most innovative startups struggle to hold on to their agility as they grow larger: "There are bright flashes of these businesses that last five to twenty-five years and then are gone. The great challenge is, as scales increase, to maintain an innovative, disruptive culture. Because someone is going to eat you up. You want it to be *you*."

At Havas Worldwide, we work hard to maintain that sort of disruptive culture Ciancutti describes. Rather than stand by as new competitors gobble up bits and pieces of the business, we place bets on where the industry is going (oftentimes in multiple directions) and invest in that direction, whether by starting something from scratch or by buying an early leader. That is how we came to acquire, for example, crowdsourcing company Victors & Spoils. Many have asked why a big, global communications company whose greatest asset is its full-time people would back a model based on having the faceless crowd create ideas. The answer is easy: This may portend a new model for our industry, and we want to be the ones driving that change.

Ciancutti reflects on why companies tend to get rigid and unresponsive as they grow in scale: "You get bigger; you have more at stake. Your people become entrenched. All these things calcify around the way your company works now. You become more averse to risk. So you add processes to manage risk. The problem is, this does not just blunt bad outcomes; it blunts the good outcomes, too. It normalizes outcomes. You become less spectacularly good... and bad." The occasional failure—even what Ciancutti calls "extra-spectacular failures"— is vital if companies are to innovate, but these become "more expensive as you grow." During his years at Netflix, he deeply admired "the way that company built a culture to be very open to change, and not risk-averse."

Steve Forbes says it is difficult not to ossify as one grows: "When you reach scale, you have to have established procedures to get things done. And the danger is getting mired down." He points to the career of Steve Jobs, who drew an important lesson from a hidebound rival:

> He looked at Sony and regarded it as a cautionary tale. They were once nimble, had a great product, then started to stagnate; there was this growth of fiefdoms. Jobs responded to that. He designed the new Apple headquarters in a way that forced people to interact; even in where he placed the restrooms, he was fostering these interactions. And in hiring decisions, if they were major decisions, positions of very real responsibility, he made sure it was not just the software department or the parts department, but that everyone would weigh in on it, so you couldn't have fiefdoms. Where Apple really took off was with the iPod. And the iPod really should have developed out of the Sony Walkman!

Ed Zschau is a former Silicon Valley CEO and U.S. congressman. In our conversation, he said he sees little hope for large companies to become more entrepreneurial, "especially those companies that promote from within; they have an inbreeding that makes it hard for them to change their spots." Like Ciancutti, he has had a ringside seat at Silicon Valley. He arrived there in 1961 and considers today's adaptive model to be one of the Valley's most important legacies, perhaps even more important than the engineering breakthroughs. "The technologies will change and become obsolete. But this idea that life is about doing new things, not just keeping doing the same things"—that is permanent. Zschau's phrase about life and novelty is a good summation of what the new, adaptive workplace is all about.

SANDBAGGING AND PREDICTABILITY

Karen Drexler, cofounder and active chair of CellScape Corporation, has had painful experience with big corporations that do not understand these new realities: the heightened need for creativity and fanning the entrepreneurial flames. Many large companies give lip service to the new trends, but, Drexler says, "I don't think they have a clue how to do it."

Here is her story: When she graduated from Stanford business school, she faced a life choice. "I really wanted to work at a company where I could have an impact," and so she passed up lucrative opportunities with consulting and venture capital firms to focus on an area she felt passionate about: the monitoring of diabetes, which runs in her family. She helped to build up a company called LifeScan, which revolutionized medicine with a new technology, the One Touch blood glucose monitoring system. Eventually, that small firm was bought by a large corporation, which then proved unhelpful during a turbulent phase when LifeScan needed patience and encouragement.

"Executives descended and said, 'We are here to help,'" Drexler remembers. "They changed the culture overnight as soon as the first goal was missed. We went from a culture of innovation to sandbagging and predictability. Innovation was gone. Gone were stretch goals so people would reach farther. They wanted goals we could make. There was a massive swap out of senior management people."

When you wreck the culture in this way, Drexler says, "People back off. They are no longer trying new things, because that is not being rewarded. Soon they fall asleep at the switch. Creative people start leaving because they are not having fun." It became clear that the big corporation's attitude toward innovation was "'these are great ideas that look interesting, but we cannot invest in that. It is too great a risk.' So innovation and risk-taking diminished quickly." Compared with the original, small company, "The priorities were very different. It was all about predictability: predict what we could deliver, then deliver it."

Ultimately, she left the business she had nurtured and believed in, concluding that big companies will never be entrepreneurial. "Innovation will continue to happen. It will happen in small companies. And big companies that want innovation will acquire it."

INNOVATION DISINCENTIVIZED

"Large companies are really unwieldy," says Jim Crawford of TRIAD Capital Management. "All these layers have to be informed when a decision is made—you have got to involve all the constituents. Lots of people would like input." But there is more to their rigidity than that: Large companies actually disincentivize their employees from being adaptive. "You can make a lot of money if you get to the top of the large company," Crawford explains, "so you try to make no enemies on the way up, to take a political approach. This is a very rational set of considerations for an ambitious young executive, but it can obscure what is best for the business." Crawford sees a striking difference at smaller organizations, where the rewards at the top are not so disproportionate and where "everybody is focused on what's best for the company."

DEFENDERS OF THE STATUS QUO

In the experience of Frank Biondi, veteran CEO of Universal Studios, Viacom, and HBO, big companies are dangerously slow to innovate. "Bureaucracies are the real enemy of new ideas," he says. "Every little bureaucrat is safe. When new ideas come along and companies have breakthroughs, the bureaucrats are defending the status quo: 'It worked in the past....'"

He goes so far as to predict that today's biggest companies are probably doomed. "If you look at the Dow in 1910, only one of those companies is still around. Little organizations have nothing to lose; they are willing to take risks. Larger organizations take too few risks, and they are constantly being eaten away by new competition. Most old-line businesses tend to get left behind." He has seen this pattern up close. Years ago, he put HBO on an RCA satellite at a time when the networks refused to consider using space-based transmission, fearing slight diminishment of the visual image. "They stayed away for years, as the whole cable industry grew on satellite."

Biondi gives an example of how failure to empower new talent produced, in one case he witnessed, a disastrous result:

> In the music business in the mid-1990s, there were smart people who understood what digital was likely to do to the existing, CD-based business, but they were junior; they reported to an old-time executive. And those people were woefully unequipped to deal with it when some smart kid said, "Here is what digital is going to do to our business." So they hired McKinsey and paid millions for a report. And when the report came it said, "The kid was right... and by the way, eight months have gone by and the whole world has changed in the meantime."

EVERY WORKER AN ENTREPRENEUR

So what do you have to do to avoid the pitfalls of MegaCorp? A big part of the solution lies in how we think about the individuals who make up our companies. Optimizing business growth in the new economy will require the full participation and creative contribution of every employee, not just those formally charged with innovation. Smart companies are finding ways to encourage and empower every worker to stimulate change and add value. We are moving toward what I expect will be an age of near-universal entrepreneurship.

This is beginning to take shape in all sorts of organizations. As Steve Forbes puts it, "Companies have made great strides lately in 'intrapreneur-ship,' cultivating the nimble spirit inside. It is a thing 3M has done for years—Post-its and the like; there you are expected to come up with something, all the time." This is something we have been experimenting with at Havas Worldwide as well. At some of our companies, people are allowed to spend 10 percent of their time on their own entrepreneurial projects against a reduction of 5 percent in salary. As we support them in turning those ideas into viable businesses, we then enable them to share the profits generated by the business in equal parts. We find that in the companies in which we offer this, a significant proportion of our talent are prepared to take the risk because often the biggest barrier to entrepreneurship is the isolation and lack of support from either financial or management partners. While this could be seen as a distraction from our core mission, I have found that people who have the ambition and aptitude to be entrepreneurial on the side typically are already overdelivering in their day jobs.

The truth is, everyone has to be creative no matter what industry they are in. The most successful people, and our most successful companies, practice what I refer to as "purposeful blurring"—meaning that creativity, or even strategy, becomes the domain (at the appropriate time) of the entire group, not just of select individuals. Involving lots of people in the creative process is incredibly important, and we are always looking to broaden the pool of ideas. When it comes to creating a brand's positioning, for instance, it is traditional to have the strategic planning group go off and do research and come back with the answer. I encourage a more dynamic and inclusive approach. For instance, on a recent assignment for a well-known consumer brand, we had our planners, creative team, and account people go to Texas to live for a week in a small community with our target consumer. For a short time, they became part of the social fabric. What they came back with was not a mere brief but a holistic plan for how the brand could add value to the consumers' lives and thereby be more meaningful.

IT STARTS WITH HIRING

To create a company that is relentlessly creative and entrepreneurial, you have to start at the beginning—with hiring. In my conversations, four essential attributes emerged that seem especially usefull now. When choosing someone new, you should ask yourself:

- Do they get it? Do they understand, at the gut level, that conditions have changed profoundly in the workplace and that a completely new approach is required?

- Are they broad? Is their background varied or, at a minimum, do they display a penchant for thinking about the big picture?
- Are they driven? What motivates them—is there an internal hunger for achievement and growth?
- Will they push us? Is this the kind of employee who will challenge the company to expand its horizons?

Do They Get It?

When I asked Steve Forbes what his talent formula is, he replied, "We find key people who get it, and we let them have responsibility to move forward with it. People who understand it is a new era and that what you know today is going to change tomorrow." Does he hand down a directive regarding what he is looking for in talent? "No, because that would lead to checklists, and checklists lead to problems."

Instead, he says, "Businesses must always remind themselves, 'What is their purpose? What are they trying to do?'—whether the means change or not. Well today, the means have changed drastically. I am looking for someone who knows, intellectually or instinctually, that it is a very much changed environment in terms of not only content creation but marketing as well."

We are all, Forbes implies, living through a revolution: "Talent—almost the definition of the word—has changed lately. It is not just the ability to do specific things anymore, but who has the mindset to get around what may have worked four years ago but is not adequate to what needs to be done today. The old attitudes won't cut it anymore."

Are They Broad?

Breadth is a critical skill today, says Arra G. Yerganian, chief marketing officer at the University of Phoenix. What does he look for when hiring? "People who are well balanced and have not spent all their time on one myopic view of their own world. Instead, they have been in different industries, have had different experiences in society. Leadership demands individuals who are very open-minded and who can break away from the 'sea of sameness.'" He cites fear as the primary cause of this homogeneity: "Fear of failing, of taking risks; fear of the societal view if you make the wrong decision."

The value of the broad-minded candidate is a topic of immense interest to Rob Price, chief marketing officer of CVS/pharmacy. His company, he says, is very complex and diverse in the services it provides, and even the smallest functional decision can have a great impact on customers. So it is critically important that they make decisions with a broad view of how customers might be affected, whether that involves, for example, changing signage and advertising or providing information about vaccinations. As a consequence, Price says, "We assess our team's ability to ask the questions that are not obvious. Can there be a customer outcome that was not thought through? We look for curiosity in our people, for people who see analogies when shopping at other types of stores. People who are imaginative, not afraid to ask a stupid question and who are optimistic enough to see through early resistance to a nontraditional idea. The ability to demonstrate critical thinking and to use data and insight to inform and improve a critical decision. People who are able to articulate how they solved a problem."

Are They Driven?

If you want to work for Steve Forbes, you had better be one of those who "doesn't wait for deadlines." "Now," he says, "it is much more about self-starting." At San Francisco State University, professor of management John Sullivan also emphasizes this all-important motivation from within. "Companies need agile, adaptable people, innovators. But these are rare." Certainly you want to bring on board the kind of person who is inwardly driven, he stresses, giving the example of an employee who quit his job not because he was not being paid well but because he was not given enough work to do. Sullivan admires this, adding, "Who wants to work in a place where he will stagnate and do nothing? 'I'm a football player,

I want to be in the game!' These are the people who make the difference. It is easy to hire average people, Homer Simpsons. It is harder to hire the better types, the Michael Jordans; it is very expensive, and they are hard to find. But an innovator will perform 300 times more than the average person. Innovators are constantly engaged. They don't need doughnuts or even money. Money is not the driver."

It is not easy to find these self-starters. At the University of Phoenix, Yerganian observes that many talented people in the workforce fail to advance their careers for reasons that he attributes to something inward. "Many people are resistant to step up, although they have the talent. Many lack that chromosome to just take the ball and run with it. So many people languish, and you wonder why. I think it is something deep within."

Will They Push Us?

The type of employee who is needed now is the driver, says Elizabeth Zea of JUEL Consulting, who assists marketing leadership nationwide in the areas of strategy, structure, and executive recruiting. The driver is someone who can both visualize change and then execute it: "You are looking for the caveman with the flint in his hand who then figures out how to create the spark."

Few entertainment companies are more admired than DreamWorks Animation SKG, where Bill Damaschke works as chief creative officer, surely one of the most coveted jobs in the world. The goal at DreamWorks, as he described it to me, is "to do things at a very high creative level and have it be a great place to work." They are distinctive for having no "house style" of movie: "We are always pushing the bar with every film," Damaschke says. "One of the real strengths of the company is that we do not want to make the same movie over and over. We value creativity and collaboration and flexibility, people who are excited about pushing themselves and their colleagues and therefore the company forward." Of potential hires he always asks, "Will they push us?"

Damaschke brings up an important point: If you only hire people who will contribute to your current competencies, you will never push past those competencies. You will pay a steep price if you make the all-too-common mistake of only hiring for your current needs rather than your future ambitions.

MARCHING TO THEIR OWN DRUMMERS

Once you have hired these forward-thinking employees, you need to treat them differently from how you might have in the past. This new breed demands freedom—and more than a little patience. You might not always understand them as they follow their own creative paths, but you want to be sure you are not hindering their natural instincts and development.

Starbucks CEO Howard Schultz has been quoted as saying, "I believe in the adage: Hire people smarter than you and get out of their way."[2] That can be tough advice to follow when self-starter talent are always bumping up against your processes, forever questioning and looking for new and better ways to do things. The last thing you want to do is strew unnecessary obstacles in the way of these adaptive, freethinking types. And that happens all too often, according to Colin Coulson-Thomas of Great Britain's University of Greenwich, who undertook a five-year study of corporate practices in human resource management. "The company's official way of doing things is often not the most effective approach. And sometimes, the people whose approaches are a better way of doing something have actually been marked down—they've actually had bad reviews, and they've been criticized for not using the corporate process."[3] That sort of obstructionism is one of the primary differentiators between companies incessantly stuck in a rut and those boldly pioneering new markets.

WHAT MILLENNIALS BRING

If the goal is to encourage entrepreneurship among your employees, you may find that millennials have an edge. Their entrepreneurial spirit runs deep: Two-thirds of U.S. colleges and universities now offer a course in entrepreneurship, and in 2011, 16 percent of new graduates started a business upon leaving college, according to a survey by the Association of Business Schools, up from 5 percent in the early 1990s.[4]

We hear a lot about the millennial penchant for multitasking, but I think even greater value lies in their tendency to tinker and hack their way around problems. Throughout history, product ideas typically have started out with a person being frustrated by something or feeling something was missing in his or her life, and then figuring out a way of fixing it. That is how we ended up with everything from the disposable diaper to earmuffs. The same applies today, with the crucial difference being that the problem and its solution are likely to be digital. Here millennials have a big head start.

Consider just one example: Marco Ament, born in 1980, kept discovering long, interesting articles online, but he didn't have time to peruse them during the workday. He wanted to read them later on his phone, so he tinkered together a solution, and Instapaper was born ("A Simple Tool to Save Web Pages for Reading Later"). It now sells as an app and generates a steady living for its inventor.

That is just one instance among thousands of this new generation's habit of doing-it-themselves. Accustomed to seeing people their own age—or even younger—coming up with smart ideas and turning them into successful products, millennials expect to troubleshoot problems and jimmy around with things to find solutions, and they also expect their superiors at work to support such endeavors.

DIFFERENT CAN BE BETTER

I talked at length about millennials with Daniel Maree, himself a millennial and also a senior global digital strategist at Havas Worldwide. He said:

> *Where we get the bad rap from the other generations is, a lot of what we do is misunderstood because it's different from how they acted and behaved. If we want to work from home, that's seen as lazy. But we are ten times more*

productive at home, because all our technology is there, and that's where we are more comfortable. Or if we ask for a raise in six months instead of waiting for two years, that's because we are building our own companies, we are very entrepreneurial; why should we be slowed down because we're now in an institutional environment? We're always looking to grow and do the next thing. That can scare some people, sometimes.

Maree notes that his peers believe they have a definite technological edge over the older generations. "Millennials feel they can operate more efficiently and smarter than older counterparts who are not so hip to the new app or gadget that streamlines your work life. We consume so much content every day, and we have a real notion of how that can improve what we do in the workplace." Highly talented millennials such as himself are being besieged by recruiters, he says. "We have a very clear sense of our value, and we aren't afraid to ask for what we want."

Going forward, you will want to create the sort of company and culture where these bright minds will find a welcoming home for their entrepreneurial aptitudes. As the next chapter will explore, engineering your workplace for constant innovation is a key step in this ongoing process.

QUESTIONS TO ASK YOURSELF

- How is your company set up to embrace change, rejecting inertia and the status quo?
- Is your size gumming up the works of change? What needs to happen to cut through the ossification and make you more agile?
- How could you better reward innovation and freethinking?
- What are you doing to ensure you are hiring self-starters who will push you in new directions? What needs to change to bring in even more adaptive talent?

CHAPTER 9

CREATE AN INNOVATION-CENTERED WORKPLACE

GETTING THE RIGHT PEOPLE IN PLACE IS AN ESSENTIAL step, but it is only the first one. Now you have to structure your workplace and processes to combat stasis and ensure a constant surge of innovative thinking and profitable ideas.

Each year, *Fast Company* puts out a list of what it considers to be the world's most innovative companies. In 2013, that list included a broad variety of organizations in a range of sizes and a wide swath of industries.[1] Although there was certainly ample representation of techie startups (Splunk, Square, Fab, Uber, Pinterest, and Airbnb, among them), there were also names that stretch as far back as the nineteenth century (Corning, Coca-Cola) and to the early years of the twentieth (Target, originally founded in Minneapolis as Dayton Dry Goods Company, and Ford Motor Co.).

How is it that these companies have managed not just to survive but also to be leaders in innovation more than a century after they were founded? And how can companies the sheer size of Ford (166,000 employees) and Coca-Cola (146,000 employees) possibly make the "most innovative" list?

The answer lies in how these organizations choose and use talent. The companies pushing the talent revolution forward have at least three qualities in common:

- They embrace a diversity of ideas.
- They encourage debate.
- They accept failure.

VITAL ELEMENTS OF THE ENTREPRENEURIAL WORKPLACE

DIVERSITY OF IDEAS

One of the things that is absolutely key to shaping strong cultures and performance outcomes is the diversity of a company's leadership team, not just in terms of gender, ethnicity, background, and experiences, but, most important, in how they think. When you bring more diverse thoughts together, the ideas you produce are more robust. The senior executives we surveyed seem to agree: 83 percent consider diversity of background and opinion in management teams a key predictor of business success.[2]

To Walt Freese, what is important is "diversity of everything. Diversity of introvert versus extrovert, information-process-oriented versus intuitive/creative, a variety of problem-solving styles—all this makes for a better organization. Because we all try to be open-minded, but we all bring our own history and personality and lens. So the more you are stretched to look at opportunities and challenges from a variety of perspectives, the more likely you will be to find bold solutions."

Like Freese, I appreciate the value of varying perspectives in crafting solutions, and I also believe diversity of thought is essential to the creative process in general. In the communications industry, we love all kinds of ideas, from lofty to mundane, plausible to outlandish. I have used a quote from chemist Linus Pauling in a number of client presentations over the years: The best way to get good ideas "is to have a lot of ideas [and then] throw away the bad ones."[3] Why not consider every possibility? You never know where the next great idea will pop up.

FREEDOM TO DEBATE

Once you get a thousand ideas floating around, you need to start puncturing some of them with a sharp needle. Because this is the necessary corollary to encouraging freethinking: You need to follow that up with critical analysis and lively debate. Is your company a place where everyone feels free to suggest ideas but also to speak up and argue against ideas that seem unproductive or ill advised? Are you encouraging a culture of debate? Maybe we all need to create a position like the one, as we saw, Sam Cicotello holds at The Motley Fool: chief rabblerouser of the highest order. Her job description: "Chief learning officer, chief rabblerouser, professional boat rocker, envelope pusher, and brain expander."[4]

Mellody Hobson of Ariel Investments described to me how her company strives, every day, for a culture of unfettered and constant debate, where even new employees are free to speak right up. "Ariel is an extraordinarily diverse organization," she says, "and that can create friction. But disagreeing with colleagues is a good thing. If we all think it is a good idea, well, we need that person to say, 'This seems too good to be true. What's wrong with this?' Groupthink is not what you are looking for in investment."

Far from wishing for less debate and discussion, Hobson would like more of it, lamenting that a quality often in short supply in the American workforce is bravery: "I think courage is lacking in a lot of organizational structures. People fear speaking their minds. There is nothing worse than after a meeting, there is all this water-cooler chatter, and I think, 'What didn't you say in the meeting that you are saying now? What didn't you say in the room where it really matters?'"

THE EMBRACE OF FAILURE

If the goal is real progress and innovation, you simply have to be brave, and that includes risking failure. Failures are as much a part of the creative process as inspiration. Scientists and technical types know this very well. James Dyson has described the inventor's life as "one of failure": "I made 5,127 prototypes of my vacuum before I got it right. There were 5,126 failures. But I learned from each one. That's how I came up with a solution. So I don't mind failure."[5] And today there is even FailCon, a conference for technology entrepreneurs, investors, developers, and designers where they study their own and others' failures to prepare for future success.[6]

In the world of business, openness to failure first took broad hold— like so many modern traits—in Silicon Valley. Jim Crawford of TRIAD Capital Management was an early observer of this Bay Area phenomenon: "When I first got into private equity, I spent lots of time in Silicon Valley, and I was struck by the fluidity of the business relationships out there. The fact that people all were networking and knew each other. All these ideas were bubbling about what was the Next Big Thing." Experts worked together, moved apart, came back together again. "If they had been in a failed business, it almost did not matter. A good idea could pull together a management team in no time. And failure was no blot on your career."

In your own business, it seems to me there are two questions you need to ask yourself:

- Do my employees know that it is OK to make mistakes in the pursuit of innovative outcomes?
- Do we make swift recovery from failure a top priority?

Creating the Safe-to-Fail Environment

As in so much else, DreamWorks has the right idea: "The company is entrepreneurial and excited about creating new things," says chief creative officer Bill Damaschke. "I love people who come from a place of 'yes'—I say, find the ten reasons an idea could work, not the one reason it would not. We tolerate failure here because you may have to fail to get to the right thing. People feel safe here."

Creating that safe feeling is not always easy, reports Peter Bregman, chief executive of Bregman Partners, a global management-consulting firm that advises CEOs. "Many senior people I know are frustrated that their direct reports are risk averse," he says. "The CEOs that I know tend to be aggressive and want aggressive people working for them; they want people to take smart risks—not stupid risks, but smart risks." But employees sometimes are hesitant to be entrepreneurial "because they are afraid of being slammed for failing in a risk and losing their job or their credibility."

What can CEOs do to encourage entrepreneurship? "Share stories about times that employees took risks and succeeded. And if they failed, how they were still supported anyway," Bregman says. For example, tell a story about a failed effort that was followed by giving the person an even bigger project to run. It is not so much a failure as it is taking a bet and one time losing the bet. Next time, he or she just might win.

In a similar vein, I asked Youngsuk Chi, chairman of the publishing giant Elsevier, "Why aren't more companies successful in fostering an entrepreneurial spirit in their employees?" He replied, "It takes two hands to make the sound of a clap. You have got to have employees willing to try new things...and a system that encourages them to do so." Insufficient time is a major obstacle to being entrepreneurial, he adds: "You are asking them to try new things, and yet having to do everything else they have to do—that is not fair."

At Elsevier, the C-suite routinely tells employees, "Do get daring. Fail often. But fail early." Because the cost of early failure is relatively small: It is like forgetting something in the house and walking back up the driveway to get it, Chi says, versus forgetting something in the house and having to drive all the way home from work for it.

He notes that there is often employee resistance, in many organizations, to the idea that they should be more entrepreneurial "because they fear punishment for failing. They don't trust us. They are afraid we will say, 'You just spent $300,000 on a prototype, and it is not work-ing!' " He has been on the receiving end of this kind of criticism many times in his career, having worked for seven companies. Executives can do much more to demonstrate a track record of entrepreneurialism, he says: "If an employee sees six other people were encouraged to fail again, that sends a very different signal from if six desks are suddenly empty next to him."

TurboTax maker Intuit has gone so far as to publicly reward failures: In 2005—on stage and in front of some 200 Intuit marketers—chairman Scott Cook presented an award to the team behind the ill-conceived RockYourRefund.com marketing campaign. The campaign had been a total bomb, but, said Cook to the assembled crowd, "It's only a failure if we fail to get the learning."[7]

Are You Set Up to Recover?

Many people I spoke with stressed the importance of speedy, intelligent recovery from failure. As in all things associated with being adaptive, this one is tricky. In encouraging employees to innovate, seasoned media CEO Frank Biondi says, "You cannot just turn people loose. The devil is in the details of *managed risk-taking*. And I think only 10 percent of companies do it well."

One key to recovery lies in taking full responsibility for failure. Longtime ExxonMobil executive Stewart McHie explains, "As companies get flatter, we need people with integrity, with self-confidence, who will take risks and take responsibility. It is OK to fail—just take responsibility, and give credit to others when things do work out."

John Sculley—former president of Pepsi-Cola Co. and, subsequently, CEO of Apple—agrees: "Being a leader in a disruptive company is a lot about recovery," he says. "It is a thin line between success and failure. A lot of time is spent in recovery, as much as in creating new stuff. Now some people have this skill, and some do not. New entrepreneurs do not realize that the majority of their life is going to be spent in recovery mode."

Today, Sculley is focused on sharing his considerable life experience with corporate executives, serial entrepreneurs, and third-wave companies that are not afraid to take risks, to adapt to change, and to use bold technological advances to achieve their goals. What counts as third-wave companies? They are not just high-tech outfits, Sculley explains, but all kinds of companies that display an ability to transform their products and organizations in response to rapid changes in the economy, social habits, or customer interests. First-wave companies were built in the agricultural age. Second-wave companies were built for growth; hence, their strength lies in their innate stability. In contrast, the strength of third-wave companies lies in change. These are what Sculley calls "the adaptive companies." He is currently working with a handful of startups that are using advanced digital technology to produce wellness-related tools—tools that have the potential to decrease dramatically the $2.5 trillion spent annually on healthcare in the United States.

ACCENTUATING THE POSITIVE AT
HAVAS WORLDWIDE LONDON

Fostering a workforce willing to take risks and able to recover quickly from disappointments is essential in my own industry. As Russ Lidstone, CEO of Havas Worldwide London, has observed, "Advertising is a business built on developing ideas where 80 percent of those ideas will end up being cut. This makes it a tough environment to work in, made tougher still by economic conditions and a rapidly changing media landscape. The net effect can be greater stress, which is why resilience is an increasingly important factor for success."

To give his talent an edge, Lidstone has set out to create a virtuous circle of positivity to boost levels of happiness, well-being, and resilience among his 240 employees in London and Manchester—with the ultimate aim of helping them be more creative. He has hired consultant Professor Neil Frude to put the entire staff at both offices through a four-week training course in "positive psychology." The intent, says Lidstone, is to

generate "both a healthier outlook and better output for us all—as a business and also at a personal level—by getting the best out of ourselves
and each other." He anticipates a "wave of little interventions across the
agency over time" to ensure lasting benefits.[8]

Establishing the sort of environment in which talent are not just
individually supported but also are encouraged to support each other is
vital to an unfettered creative process.

ENCOURAGING THE ENTREPRENEURIAL EMPLOYEE

How does one engender an entrepreneurial climate among workers at all
levels and in all functions? "It is hard to create that culture," says Randy
Altschuler, executive chairman of CloudBlue. "Every month we recognize
somebody. We reward people. I don't think companies can put a big enough
emphasis on this. You need to make it clear: 'If you want to advance within
the company, being innovative is the way to do this.'" What are the typical
obstacles to building this kind of culture? I asked. "People don't think it
will matter to their own career. Some employees are not necessarily looking
to spend lots of overtime; they are here to earn a paycheck. You must make
it clear to them that there are real rewards to being entrepreneurial."

But too many companies are sending the wrong signal. Frank Biondi
says the reason there is so little bold innovation in general is that "most companies are really rewarded for doing what they do, only better: Dropping the
cost of detergent. Making the factory run at 90 percent instead of 60 percent
efficiency. Dropping scrappage. These things are so hard to do well, so organizations get heavily focused on them, and the talent pool gets skewed toward
greater efficiency in established processes" instead of toward real progress.

And too often, Biondi says, if you encourage entrepreneurship
among your employees, their manager will steal the credit. "This is a tone-
from-the-top issue, if you let middle management steal ideas or quash
ideas." He concludes that entrepreneurship among employees is difficult
to attain: "Historically, people do not get rewarded for raising their hands,
especially in old-line organizations."

REWARD OFFERED

Far different from the old-line places are the exciting new firms that not only invite employees to be adaptive and innovative but give them financial backing too. CareerBuilder, which operates the largest online employment website, with 24 million unique visitors monthly, invites its employees around the world to submit an entrepreneurial idea of their choice for a chance to win $60,000 to launch their own business unit within the company. It is called the Ideas from Everywhere program. The winning concept is funded for a year, with the employee personally put in charge. CareerBuilder receives 50 to 70 ideas annually, says vice president of human resources Rosemary Haefner: "It is very intensive—write up the plan, do the research, make your case."

The advantages are numerous: "People get to take charge of their own growth and development," Haefner says. They discover more about the company and find out "what somebody else is doing in a different department" (because proposals always require some collaboration). Ideas from Everywhere encourages networking and fosters "a healthy competition that challenges everyone to raise their game."

Added to the contest last year was crowdsourcing. This enhanced the quality of the proposals because everybody in the company worldwide was watching. In addition, peers helped each other build the ideas out more fully, with the assistance of internal experts. Haefner cites one notable contest winner: a supply-and-demand portal, which applies millions of data points on job listings and active job seekers to measure the labor pressure for any occupation in any location. The portal can tell you which cities are the best places to find your desired talent, your top competitors for talent, the aggregate profiles of candidates, and more.

JUDGING IDEAS ON MERIT, NOT SENIORITY

John Ciancutti spent more than a dozen years at Netflix and praises its democratic culture, one free from the rigidities of top-down control. He told me a story that happened early in his career, back when the company's new website was arranged "like retail shelves—like detergents on the shelf at Walmart—each location chosen by experts. I saw this and I thought, 'This looks crazy to me.'" And when he logged into the website, it would show him movies that he had already watched and had no intention of watching again or movies he had no interest in at all. Moreover, the films that were featured prominently on the home page would quickly go out of stock, "so we were driving demand to titles that we couldn't fulfill. We were manufacturing customer dissatisfaction."

In his youthful innocence, Ciancutti envisioned a solution: "I wrote a simple system to decide which titles were best for which customers." Any out-of-stock titles would be hidden. "I spent a week. It was as basic as could be." He took it to CEO Reed Hastings, whose response was, "Boom, instantly, yeah, roll it out right now." No top-down control, no elaborate process.

But then came a lesson. "There was fallout with another team. We had four or five people who did this program. And the person in charge was hugely angry with me for having gone around her to the CEO. I had been naïve. That was the first moment I understood the culture here. That 'Oh, I would be in a lot of trouble in any other company; I didn't go through the proper channels, I didn't get buy-in.'" At Netflix, as modeled by the response of Reed Hastings, all that mattered were the results.

In 2013, Netflix retains its entrepreneurial culture, what Ciancutti describes as, "'Do what you think is going to be very effective.' Right now, while we are talking, they are making better and better algorithms. And when they make one, everybody applauds—even the ones who wrote the last great thing" that is about to get discarded.

FLATTEN DECISION MAKING

I spoke with Alexis Nasard, chief commercial officer at one of the world's great beer makers, about what makes his company cutting-edge in the talent field. "Heineken is very creative," he explained. "It's about brand-building and lifestyle marketing. It encourages risk-taking. We sponsored the latest James Bond film. Now, at any other company, that would have been a three-months-long process to get approval. At such places, every single idea has to be quantified, every risk assessed, and you have to align everyone... and his grandfather. At Heineken, it was a half-hour process. I went to the CEO, showed him the facts, made the case, and we went and did it."

Nasard went on to explain that creativity cannot exist within the confines of the old command-and-control structures: "At other companies, you have to justify every cent you spend on anything. Suppose you want to make a certain package a brighter color of green. That would require a deck of 700 pages explaining why. At Heineken, we just hold hands and hope for the best results. Now Heineken is not sloppy or undisciplined, but it does not have the illusion of wasting money and resources in quantifying what is not quantifiable. How are you ever going to quantify the impact on sales of James Bond drinking Heineken?"

What kills creativity is "when you put people who are not developed and bred in an understanding of the role of creativity in charge of making branding decisions. Here at Heineken, the creative types have a blast. You get to do what you are best at. A company that is creative is not dogmatic, and therefore it is more inspiring and dynamic."

TOOLS AND TECHNIQUES

It is not possible to become a fully adaptive workplace without having the tools and support structures that people need to keep their creativity humming. Innovation prompts are absolutely vital, says Dave Ulrich, a professor at the University of Michigan's Ross School of Business and partner at RBL Group: "Employees with an entrepreneurial predisposition take risks, experiment, learn, and continue to grow. Some of this passion comes from personal drive, but some can be hewn and encouraged by organization systems that allow risk-taking and encourage experimentation, learning from successes and failures, and constantly improving."

The most common tools to encourage adaptiveness may be broken down into three classes: the perpetual idea-fest, the hackathon, and time off for innovation.

THE PERPETUAL IDEA-FEST

By this term I mean, in a general sense, an institution-wide commitment to drumming up original ideas, all the time. At Whirlpool, senior vice president David Binkley explains how creativity is not hidden away in a remote lab. Instead, "we have innovation tools, processes, and methods dispersed across the organization. It gives people a lot of room to innovate. We make things, and we make a lot of them; innovation is connected to a business outcome, so it is very natural for us. We believe innovation is not just for a handful of people." Binkley cites Gladiator GarageWorks storage products as an example of a new line of business sparked by the company's idea-rich culture.

Other ongoing idea-fests in American business include:

- ZFrogs, described by Mike Bailen at Zappos as "sort of like a venture capitalist group made up of our top executives. They come together frequently to hear a pitch given by Zappos employees on things like how to improve the buying experience or company productivity. If they like what they hear, the group will provide resources to make sure that the idea can be implemented."
- DreamWorks not only actively solicits ideas from every employee but also gives them the training to pitch their ideas successfully. Dan Satterthwaite, head of HR, explains, "Whether it's an idea for a new movie or a better plan for developing new products, DreamWorks believes that stirring the creative juices is critical for keeping the international company competitive."[9]

THE HACKATHON

Here is another idea that sprang out of Silicon Valley: the hackathon. I spoke with Tomer Kagan, a young entrepreneur who started his first business in college; left a lucrative career in DNA sequencing to return to entrepreneurism; and recently founded Quixey, a company offering "a search engine for apps." Kagan described to me how hackathons work at his organization: "They are full-day, once a quarter. We have random teams, ten of them, each one interdisciplinary. Each tackles a broad problem related to our product. When given access to all internal data and tools, it is almost like having ten startup firms. Our last hackathon led to three patents."

At Facebook, Ciancutti points to their Hack Day "where anyone can roll up their sleeves and spend 24 hours building anything they want. Much of what they build, it goes straight into the product." A great deal of what Facebook now proffers has come out of these sessions.

Creative Business Ideas

The previous examples come from tech companies, but the basic idea of the hackathon is of course applicable to many kinds of organizations, not just digital and software firms. At my company, we have something called CBI Labs—they are held both internally and in conjunction with client teams.

Around a dozen years ago, some of our agency leaders got together and came to what might well have been a disturbing conclusion: Marketing communications was no longer working and would never again work if agencies continued to follow twentieth-century models of business. Fragmented audiences, splintered media, and a profusion of claims on consumers' attention were just some of the obstacles we were up against. And so we set about inventing a whole new way to do business—one based not simply on generating and communicating ideas (we had always done that) but on embedding them deep in the heart of our clients' businesses. No longer would we ask, "What's the advertising idea?" but "What's the business idea?"

At their best, these ideas would be sufficiently powerful to affect the fundamentals of the company—how it perceives itself, what it sells, its long-term strategy, the role it plays in people's lives. We ended up calling these Creative Business Ideas® (CBIs), and they have been our point of focus ever since. Over the years, we have applied CBIs to client businesses around the globe; for example, helping a bottled water company transform itself into a source of youth, enabling a car company to transcend the automotive category, and even reimagining the Paris metro system.

One of our first steps in building an agency culture around CBIs was to start a process by which we could produce more such ideas—a way to capture creative lightning on a more regular basis. We came up with the idea of CBI Labs—daylong (sometimes longer) sessions that start with the sharing of information and insights to get everyone as smart as possible about the brand in question, its category, and its consumers. We use our proprietary research tools to explore how we can increase brand relevance, magnify the brand's advantage over competitors, and exploit opportunities, including existing gaps in the market. We then work together with the client to generate a number of strategic ideas that play into the intersections identified. And, finally, we agree on, articulate, and flesh out the single most powerful idea: the CBI.

This process—including group exercises and challenges—has now been shared across our entire network through local workshops and ongoing support from the CBI training team. Maintaining a consistent approach streamlines the process and ensures the best thinking results from each ideation session, regardless of in which of our 316 offices it is held.

TIME OFF FOR INNOVATION

Lots of attention has been directed to companies giving talent time to work on projects of their own choosing. 3M and HP give certain employees up to 15 percent of their working time to develop their own ideas. Intuit offers four hours of unstructured time per week. At Google, as has been widely publicized, engineers are allowed to spend up to 20 percent of their work time on personal projects that might ultimately help the business. Several services provided by Google today, such as Gmail, Orkut, Google News, and AdSense, are said to have been invented by employees during such downtime. Apple recently followed this pattern with an initiative called Blue Sky, in which select employees are invited to spend a few weeks of their time creatively.

If a day off is a good idea, why not a week or a month? After all, "Everything we know about innovation, it happens in the downtime," says Sabrina Parsons of Palo Alto Software. "That's absolutely necessary for innovation."

Some organizations are experimenting with this idea of long blocks of dedicated "thinking" time. As *Wired* recently reported, "LinkedIn is quietly offering its own take on letting workers run wild with InCubator, a program that may well top what Google offers. Under InCubator, engineers can get 30 to 90 days away from their regular work to develop ideas of their own into products. Their ideas must first be developed into prototypes and clear two rounds of judging, with founder Reid Hoffman and CEO Jeff Weiner involved in the final round. Many ideas submitted to InCubator come from LinkedIn's monthly 'hack days,' in which workers can win awards for small bits of quickly written software."[10]

In June 2012, the web-application company 37signals undertook a daring experiment, offering employees what it called "a full month of free time to think, explore, mock up, prototype, whatever." As cofounder Jason Fried explained on a company blog:

> *People can go solo or put together a team—it's entirely up to them. This is a month to unwind and create without the external pressures of other ongoing projects or expectations. We're effectively taking a month off from nonessential scheduled/assigned work to see what we can do with no schedule/assignments whatsoever. . . . So our theory is that we'll see better results when people have a long stretch of uninterrupted time. . . . The culmination of this month of free work time is Pitchday. . . . That's when everyone will get a chance to pitch their idea, mockup, prototype, or proof of concept to the whole company.*[11]

The company recognized that this experiment was risky, but the results turned out to be highly satisfactory. "How can we afford to put our business on hold for a month to 'mess around' with new ideas?" 37signals asked itself and then concluded, "How can we afford not to? We would never have had such a burst of creative energy had we stuck to business as usual. Bottom line: If you can't spare some time to give your employees the chance to wow you, you'll never get the best from them."[12]

QUESTIONS TO ASK YOURSELF

- What needs to change to make your company a place where everyone feels free to suggest ideas and speak up and argue against ideas that seem unproductive?
- What are the advantages of setting aside time for people to be paid simply to think? To imagine a new future for the company?
- What more should you be doing to reward innovation—wherever within the company it happens to reside?

CHAPTER 10

MAKE IT EASY TO COLLABORATE

Our superstars are not the high-scoring shooting guards, but the assist-passing point guards who can get the best of people around them.
—*Brian Trelstad, partner, Bridges Ventures*

BACK WHEN THE WORLD SEEMED TO CHANGE RELATIVELY slowly, a company with a winning product could maintain the status quo for decades and still be a success. Not anymore: Whoever comes up with a great new idea in our age of hyperacceleration enjoys just a few months' lead before competitors launch something even more attractive. The only way to compete in such a ruthless environment is to continually come up with killer ideas—and the only way to do that is to build an organization in which smart people can pool their insights and constantly spark off each other.

Such collaborative arrangements give a tremendous advantage to businesses that encourage cross-pollination and facilitate connections across functions, generations, and status levels—both within and outside the company. And those rewards are profoundly tangible. The IBM Global CEO Study found that companies with extensive collaboration capabilities regularly outperform the competition in both revenue growth and average operating margin.[1]

THE NEW WORLD DEMANDS—AND
REWARDS—COLLABORATION

The good news is that it is constantly getting easier and faster to bring in thinkers, business partners, and helpful outside influences. Whereas it used to be more efficient for organizations to accumulate people and resources in-house to keep transaction costs down, now cheap computing, web-based software, open-source models, and more sophisticated management approaches are rapidly reducing the costs of doing business between locations and companies. It is more rewarding than ever to look to other industries and cultures for ideas and to assemble teams with disparate views, backgrounds, and skills.

Collaboration lies at the heart of my workday every day. I spend at least 30 percent of my time interacting with our teams and partners. And I am constantly building relationships with people beyond my company, not necessarily for anything specific at the moment, but with an eye toward potentially joining forces someday. I think that is the mindset every business leader needs to maintain.

To embrace an exciting new chance to collaborate, build relationships, and learn from people in fields far removed from my own—these promising opportunities were what attracted me to the Henry Crown Fellowship program at the Aspen Institute in Washington, DC. There are 21 people in my "class" at this famous convener of leaders devoted to the consideration of broad societal problems, and I find it fascinating to hear everyone's thoughtful perspectives on a disparate array of issues. This book benefits from the insights of a number of supertalents I have gotten to know through the program, including Leighanne Levensaler (Workday), John Ciancutti (Facebook), Sheila Marcelo (Care.com), Robert Price (CVS/pharmacy), and Stephanie Tilenius (KPCB).

What I have learned, and continue to learn, from these and other experts—plus my own experiences—is that collaboration is best approached as a long-term strategy for the company, one that is actively promoted and nurtured. It is not enough to hope that connections will arise serendipitously or by the everyday interactions that take place naturally within the organization. Instead, as business leaders, we must work extremely hard to instill a culture of vigorous and daily collaboration and also to give our talent the tools and impetus they need to connect broadly and richly with others.

TOOLS AND TECHNIQUES FOR A MORE COLLABORATIVE ENVIRONMENT

It does not matter what industry you are in—every company needs to collaborate and assiduously seek out the best partners with which to dance. Business-school textbooks are littered with examples of companies that missed the boat by failing to make the right connections at the right time. As described in the *Harvard Business Review*, Sony failed to lead the MP3 revolution because its internal silos were competing; a similar lack of success owing to poor collaboration befell the tablet computer that Microsoft fumblingly developed in the early 2000s; and Daimler ended up selling Chrysler at a $35 billion loss because the engineers at the newly merged company could not envisage a way of working together.[2]

These tools and techniques should prove helpful in minimizing miscommunications, unproductive competition, and information firewalls of the kinds that impede progress at so many companies:

- Hire communicators.
- Mix things up to bring people together.
- Create "we space"... but don't forget the "me space."
- Keep people in motion.
- Expand your workforce—by making your company smaller.
- Bring the outside in.

HIRE COMMUNICATORS

Collaboration and communication plainly go hand in hand. A brilliant idea that takes shape in the mind of one person will live there forlornly unless he or she can put it into words and communicate it with eloquence and persuasiveness. Collaborating is all about passing around ideas, discussing them, building on them, and bringing them to life. Each stage requires strong communication skills.

At Vorbeck Materials, John Lettow rates communication as a vital aspect of his job. He was surprised by how much coordination it takes to make sure all necessary information reaches the full range of stakeholders. "I have a decent technical background and some business background," he says, "but, as president, I had to ensure that I was coordinating between all the groups. That was the most important part of my job! You don't realize that, jumping in: You have to communicate with everyone."

After his baptism by fire, he developed some smart practices to keep communication and collaboration going. He personally keeps staff up-to-date with a steady flow of information, but he also delegates, designating specific people to communicate with certain groups. And that critical responsibility to communicate is by no means limited to top executives—everybody throughout the company is expected to be good at shooting ideas in a variety of directions: up to management, within their team, across to other teams, out to customers.

"Every employee has a diverse stakeholder group," says Lettow. "It can be tricky." Knowing this, he is reluctant to hire anybody who does not have strong interpersonal skills: "If a person is not a good communicator, it would really limit the role he or she could have within the company."

MIX THINGS UP TO BRING PEOPLE TOGETHER

Ideas flow only sluggishly when talent find themselves confined to musty silos, glued to their workstations, made to keep to themselves all day. Things only get moving when everyone mixes in an open environment that encourages them to share and bounce concepts around informally.

Food can be a great workplace facilitator of human interactions, as Thomas Edison realized long ago. After supper at home, he would return to his lab for a nine o'clock "midnight lunch" ordered from a local tavern. Taking a break from their test tubes and electrical apparatus, his workers would eat, share ideas, swap stories, and even sing songs before getting back to the job at hand. It was a pleasurable—and effective—way for Edison to forge the sort of relationships that would facilitate the sharing of ideas and a more open approach to invention.[3]

In today's much-changed world, cloud-hosting firm Rackspace similarly finds that food is a great mixer. As Henry Sauer told us, the company gets a dozen or more gourmet food trucks to pull up outside the office every Tuesday and Friday. "We have a huge party tent outside, with picnic tables, and you'll see 300 or 400 Rackers mixing and mingling and making connections. There is a lot of opportunity for people to interact."

Mixing the generations is an important exercise at The Weather Company, chairman and chief executive David Kenny told me. A big challenge today is "getting millennials to stop and learn from their elders." For example, the company has been forecasting the weather for many years, "but new people come in and think, 'I know how to reinvent this.' And they don't know what mistakes were already made in past such efforts. So they take a big step backwards." His solution: to have meetings of both generations. "Let's take an afternoon and look at what works and what doesn't. It is hard work to mix them. They have got to leave their egos at the door; you have got to make people feel safe. But if you can do it, it's awesome."

Kenny is making an effort to blend the culture of the traditional firm with the newest innovations and the freshest perspectives from young talent. He thinks it's a mistake when companies "run digital and traditional separately." When you do that, he says, "you don't get the best answer. You get two answers."

Getting people to mix and interact becomes a more difficult matter as companies grow. When Bill Damaschke joined DreamWorks Animation, he was just the fortieth employee; now the company numbers around 2,000. "We call where we work the Campus," he told me. "It is a beautiful

Spanish Mediterranean setting. We serve breakfast and lunch every day, and community happens." And DreamWorks takes still further steps to encourage interaction; for example, offering classes relevant to the company's work—focusing on topics such as painting, photography, ideas-pitching, and camera and composition. Not only do individuals develop their skills through these classes, but they also link up with types of people they might not otherwise meet.

Go Off-Campus

Even in the liveliest offices, things can gradually grow inward-looking and claustrophobic. Zappos believes that occasionally going outside the workplace to connect with co-workers is important, so it encourages managers to spend a good chunk of their time beyond the bounds of the four walls of headquarters. At the San Francisco–based cloud-storage company Dropbox, they have found a simple way of getting hard-pressed coders to decompress together: informally scrambling up a nearby hilltop, a ritual they call Hillcore. The brisk ascent allows ideas to be discussed and fresh insights gained. Expanding the tradition, one team went stalking through a cornfield in Illinois, an outing that produced the kernel of a useful idea concerning passwords.[4]

Whether the mixing happens on-site or outside the office, it doesn't always have to be about work. The Nerdery tries hard to get solitary coders to interact and create new solutions together. As Kris Szafranski tells it, the company recognized that pockets of nerds often congregated on their own time to pursue shared interests, and so they decided to get behind that as a company: "We have become more visually supportive of this and now have more than 20 Nerdery clubs—everything from game development to loose-leaf tea to wellness (or WellNerds)."

CREATE "WE SPACE"...BUT DON'T FORGET THE "ME SPACE"

As we often hear about, companies that aim to foster collaboration are quickly moving away from traditional office setups to workspaces that offer plenty of common ground. David Binkley tells of how Whirlpool recently rebuilt its office environment to be far more open: "We have 'we space,' not 'me space,' huddle rooms, places for chance encounters. It fosters agility and fast learning and collegiality."

Companies heavy on communal space need to ensure there is also ground for employees who need an enclave for focused introspection and quiet. That may mean working from home or using "getaway rooms." Collaboration drives innovation, but focused, uninterrupted time is when things most efficiently get done. "When you have a long stretch when you aren't bothered, you can get in the zone," says the 37signals book *Getting Real*. "The zone is when you are most productive. It's when you don't have to mindshift between various tasks. It's when you aren't interrupted to answer a question or look up something or send an email or answer an im [instant message]. The alone zone is where real progress is made."[5]

Fostering Collaboration at Our New Headquarters

At Havas Worldwide, everything we do as an agency network is centered on producing brilliant ideas for clients, and so we take collaboration seriously. Over the past year or so, we have invested in consolidating our business, creative, and media teams within some of our hubs (Paris, Chicago, Boston, Shanghai, and elsewhere) to make it easier to exchange information and ideas. In 2013, we are doing the same at our world headquarters, bringing together the majority of our New York–based agencies onto a new campus.

Here is our approach: We have constructed our workspace to maximize light and visibility. There are virtually no walls, all furniture and coloring is light and bright, and there is abundant natural hardwood and plenty of greenery. Moreover, we have organized our space into three zones: personal, private, and public.

- Personal: Everyone has his or her own workspace at a table
  with 12 to 16 team members. Rather than think in terms of

independent departments, we cross-pollinate; all of the positive influences for a given business are gathered together on a single part of the floor. We believe this hybrid model allows our employees to interact easily with the people they most closely work with on projects while also gaining the benefit of other peers and influencers nearby.

- Private: Each floor offers a number of "huddle rooms," quiet spots for those who need to get away from the buzz of the agency and conceptualize, talk, think, or just take a breather—no reservations required.
- Public: We have nearly 100 meeting rooms across the building that range from smaller team rooms to large client conference rooms. In addition, we have open seating around all the floors for impromptu reviews and chats, including the much-appreciated living rooms outfitted with PlayStations for occasional breaks.

From the Genius Bar for IT support to the on-site production facility and open café area, we have taken much consideration in designing the space to suit our needs. Gone are the days of closed doors and private meetings. Creativity is a team sport, and we have provided our players with the best equipment and the best environment.

KEEP PEOPLE IN MOTION

In times gone by, clunky, deskbound telephones and massively immovable filing cabinets—not to mention hierarchical corporate mindsets—kept employees in their place, both figuratively and literally. Now, of course, wireless communications and less rigid workplaces foster flexible mentalities. As discussed earlier, The Motley Fool is one of a growing number of organizations embracing a philosophy of trusting employees to know what is best for them and their personal work, and that includes as basic a matter as where to sit. Every Fool has a desk with wheels, so employees who need to collaborate simply roll their desks together; a person who needs alone time can shift off to a quiet spot.[6]

At Care.com, they have the Sheila Shuffle—named in honor of founder and CEO Marcelo—whereby they bump everybody to a different desk annually. "It's about embracing change, about evolving, about having less turfyness. There are no walls in this office. You have new neighbors every year," Marcelo explains. The Shuffle emerged in response to employees showing a propensity to clump into predictable groups: Men and women weren't mixing much, nor were the various foreign-born staffers. "When you move their desks every spring, new people start having lunch together," Marcelo says. "It helps them learn what everybody is doing; you see what they are working on." Today, the Care.com office boasts a glass-walled kitchen right in the middle, so everybody sees the constant comings and goings. And in case that is not enough, bagels are delivered every Friday, but always to a different floor. As a result, "You meet in stairwells and break rooms: it's a nice impromptu chance to talk."

EXPAND YOUR WORKFORCE—BY MAKING YOUR COMPANY SMALLER

None of us can afford to make less-than-optimal use of anyone in our employ. The competition is simply too great nowadays, our resources stretched too thin. And yet we are all doing it, especially those of us who have sizable workforces spread over scores of offices. Critical communications too often are not shared among offices, and the best insights and ideas may lie hidden from everyone who is not fortunate enough to be in some favored location. The good news is that all of this is beginning to change, albeit slowly, as companies get smarter about using available collaboration tools to create virtual workspaces in which employees can gather and exchange thoughts.

Make It Easy to Share Information

However far-flung your employees may be, smart use of new technologies can allow everybody to spark ideas off one another. But it is surprising how businesses have generally been slower than individuals to make full use of social networking. After all, we know that just about everyone we work with is on one social network or another; why not apply the concept to our organizations? Belatedly, more companies are doing just that: investing in their own internal networks, allowing their talent to communicate with colleagues on the other side of the building—or the other side of the planet—in much the same way as they chat with friends and family on Facebook.

The official name for this game is enterprise social networking. Salesforce.com's Chatter is just one example. GE has its own system—GE Colab—created to deliver the sorts of rich benefits employees have come to expect in their private social-media lives: quick responses and the ability to reach out to folks they see in person only infrequently, if ever. According to GE Corporate's chief information officer, Ron Utterbeck, the core of Colab is a Facebook-like function called Stream, which shows its users (115,000 as of late 2012) all the activity of friends, the groups they have joined, and where they are located. There is also a file-sharing capability.

Colab fills a critical need, it seems. "We're a pretty collaborative culture to begin with," Utterback told *MIT Sloan Management Review*, "but some of our challenges, as we're global, is how do you connect people? How do we make it so that you can search and get the right skill sets very easily? How do you make GE a lot smaller of a place?"

As Colab functionality has grown, a surge in healthy new collaboration has enabled employees to solve problems faster and to readily find the experts they need. Utterbeck points to an employee who might hope to bounce a certain issue off a compliance officer in faraway India—Colab allows him or her to find and instantly connect with the right individual. One in three Colab connections takes place across functions, one in four across geographies, one in five across business units. Clearly, this is a collaborative instrument of immense value.[7]

Make Use of Your Global Network

No matter how complicated it is to pull off, every organization must do all it can to share ideas and information across all its locations. Bob

O'Leary at Citi knows this all too well: "We have to be effective with the dollars," he says. "That means sharing best practices and co-creating. We cannot be reinventing the wheel all the time." International companies need to tap all their office locations for promising breakthroughs. Rather than always creating some brilliant new concept in-house, O'Leary says, employees need to look to the team in Brazil or wherever else for cutting-edge ideas. We need "to formulate solutions collectively, not individually."

At my own company, we built Havas Crowd, a technology-enabled platform that puts creative briefs out to our offices around the world. Anyone can answer the brief, applying their unique thinking, insights, and ideas. If their work is chosen by the agency that put the brief out there, the agency that provided the idea gets a fee. We are already seeing great ideas bubbling up from this, and the process is driving down our costs and our reliance on freelancers.

BRING THE OUTSIDE IN

Sun Microsystems cofounder Bill Joy is credited with formulating Joy's Law, which sums up every business leader's angst: "No matter who you are, most of the smartest people work for someone else." The question, then, is how to access the skills and knowledge base of these smart folks outside your company without attempting to hire them all.

ArnoldNYC has a program it calls Friends of the Factory (FOF). The concept behind FOF is simple, says president Lynn Power: "Admit we don't know everything. From there, the possibilities for partnership and collaboration are endless." She elaborates:

> We started the FOF program with a focus on extending the capabilities
> and skill sets that we most needed, bringing in partners that could help
> us produce our thinking on virtually any stage—and give us the benefit of
> working with different brains, learning new approaches, and giving our
> clients different solutions. From there, the program has morphed into more
> of a "bringing the outside in" philosophy. A major benefit of this philosophy

*is that it helps to create an agency mindset that is inherently open-minded,
incredibly curious, and always anticipating what's next. And it lets us create
a learning culture that does not feel like "training"; it's more organic—and
much more fun.*

Making Use of the Crowd

Of course, social media has opened up plenty of new channels for drawing
inspiration and innovations from the crowd. In 2006, Netflix announced
a competition inviting any individual or team to try to beat the company's
user-rating predictions for movies by more than 10 percent. Hundreds of
teams took part, and, after staged annual prizes, in 2009, the company
paid out the full $1 million Netflix Prize. Tellingly, the top two teams
achieved their results by joining forces with other competitors and incor-
porating their work.[8] Encouraged by this experience, in 2012, Netflix
teamed up with captioning and subtitling company Amara on a pilot
project to crowdsource the subtitling of videos.[9]

If you are not yet convinced of the value of collaborating with the
crowd, consider this: Before it was acquired by Google, YouTube had just
65 employees and yet was valued at $1.65 billion, thanks almost entirely
to crowd-generated content, from cavorting kittens to helicopter crashes
to tuneless preteen crooners.[10] In another example, Wikipedia had just five
employees in early 2007, whereas the venerable Encyclopaedia Britannica
had more than 100 full-time editors and 4,000 paid contributors. Yet
Wikipedia, famously a crowd-created resource, offers 60 times more articles than Britannica, its content is more up-to-date, and it is far more
frequently consulted. It garners 470 million unique visitors every month,
equivalent to every single person in the European Union logging on.[11]

Crowdsourcing need not necessarily involve going outside the company, as Microsoft has proved. Ahead of releasing Windows 7 in multiple
countries, it needed to ensure that the dialogue boxes worked in every
language. So the company turned the task into a game for employees. The
objective was to find as many errors as possible in the localized dialogue
boxes. There were no financial rewards, just the fun of the chase and a

little glory. This internal crowd reviewed a half-million dialogue boxes and ferreted out hundreds of language and coding errors.[12]

Sleep with the Enemy/There Are No Enemies

Even as the scramble for profits and market share grows more furious, companies are actively collaborating with competitors. Sometimes it is a matter of recognizing shared interests, such as devising common standards in opening new markets. Often it is about finding complementary interests that spark fruitful collaboration, co-creation, and partnerships.

In the old world of work, the notion of sharing anything with a competitor would instantly raise alarms. Secrecy was paramount. But now in our hyperconnected world, it has become apparent that few things can remain secret for long. Products and processes can be reverse engineered; anything digital can be copied and leaked. The value now is in the strategic sharing of information and the pooling of resources. Car makers routinely share the massive costs of developing and producing platforms as well as the subassemblies that go into the vehicles (such as brakes and safety equipment).[13] The all-important brand difference comes in the body styling, the level of finish, and (I hasten to add) the marketing.

Amazon takes the concept of a shared platform even further. Search for an item on the massive retail site, and you will often find it offered by Amazon plus a host of alternative suppliers, all on the same page. With its Marketplace retail platform, any professional third-party vendor can access Amazon's billing, marketing, distribution, and customer-relationship-management systems. By separating its production and distribution businesses, Amazon has successfully created an ecosystem of retailers that are wholly integrated into its fulfillment process. Amazon has more than two million third-party sellers worldwide who pay it a commission on sales plus a monthly membership fee. Analysts estimate that Marketplace—a spectacular example of collaborating with the competition—generates between 9 and 12 percent of Amazon's $48.1 billion annual revenue.[14]

As John Sculley pointed out to us, "This sort of collaboration started happening in the entertainment industry: There used to be one production company, but now, watch the beginning of a film and there are four to six different production companies." Today, in the wider world of business, the trend is toward bringing talent in, "in whatever structure the talent wants to come. Increasingly, talent has its own company."

More and more, it seems that the future belongs to the collaborators.

QUESTIONS TO ASK YOURSELF

- What other tools and processes need to be in place for your workers to collaborate and connect effectively across locations and functions?
- Where within your company can the "wisdom of crowds" add value?
- Where do opportunities lie for smart partnerships with other entities—including your competitors?

CHAPTER 11

HARNESS THE TIDAL WAVE OF DIGITAL

UNDERLYING EVERY ASPECT OF MODERN TALENT MAN-agement is the vast and inescapable phenomenon of the digital revolution. It has swept across the business world like a tidal wave, rewriting the talent equation along with everything else. Going forward, digital will be everywhere, in everything we touch. It will allow us to create value in new ways, to be constantly learning and acquiring new skills, and to be globally aware. It will drive a breakneck pace of change by giving talent the means to quickly create what comes next in whatever area they ply their trade. And it will put a massive premium on the qualities of insatiable curiosity and inventiveness.

As we move through this century, the people and companies that will be especially successful will be those that embrace digital, in all its fast-changing manifestations; they will be constantly learning about and through it, and they will be unflaggingly curious about what might be done with it. When iPads first came out, I remember being in client meetings with old-line companies, ones you might think would be slow to accept change, and yet everybody had their tablet, everybody was enthusiastically using and experimenting with this game-changing piece of new technology. I began to realize then that full, spirited participation in the digital revolution is now the same thing as being serious about success in the world of business. High-tech and business know-how have fused.

Are you participating fully in the revolution?

You had better get on board, cautions Elizabeth Zea of JUEL Consulting. Talking to her, one gets the impression of a life-or-death struggle in business:

> *It is back to Darwin: As digital came into the mix, there was this need to introduce new ways of thinking—ultimately to introduce a new gene pool into the marketing mix with the goal of emerging with a stronger species. To seek out and hire more evolved, digital marketers and crossbreed them with the traditional marketers. For those companies that have failed to do so, there is a limited runway in how successful they will be. We have got to crossbreed; we have got to bring in new skill sets. When your species is under threat, if you do not evolve and adapt, you become extinct.*

As I have thought about the digital revolution lately and how it is reshaping my own industry, three fundamentals come to mind, three inescapable new corollaries that I believe you need to concentrate on if you hope to be successful:

1. Everybody needs digital expertise now.
2. Amid hyperchange, everyone needs to constantly learn…and relearn.
3. The great digital divide favors forward-thinkers over fossils.

Each of these concepts deserves our careful attention.

EVERYBODY NEEDS DIGITAL EXPERTISE NOW

When Michael Powell became head of the FCC in 2001 (at age 37), he instantly realized that the agency was on the wrong side of a rapidly growing crevasse between those who were tech-savvy and those who were not. The great electronic revolution had barely begun, but Powell astutely recognized the vital importance of getting everybody on board, and quickly: "It struck me right away how dramatically the people were changing on the other side of the table from us. Here were Steve Case, Bill Gates. I quickly realized, 'We are not going to be credible if we don't have the talent skills and depth and personnel matchup with the community we are engaged with.' So I said, 'From now on, learning in this space will be a forever exercise. It is a world of continual reinvention now. I want a labor force that reinvents itself every day.' "

To make sure that learning was available right at hand, he established FCC University inside the headquarters building. Powell's mantra continues to be that talent must eagerly embrace new technology: "You have got to keep adding digital to the equation. You have to play with the tools, not just know about them."

As Powell perceived, every employee needs digital skills—no exceptions. No longer can such expertise be confined to an IT department or the digital arm of inveterate techno geeks. We all have to be geeks. It is true across every industry. Take banking, for example, where Stephen Oxman, senior advisor at Morgan Stanley, told me that new hires are increasingly comfortable with digital, which is a great relief because "much of what they are being asked to do is dependent upon their digital savvy. Being able to mine what is out there on the Internet and quickly identify key sources of information and bring them to bear, for financial analysis."

The same is true at Citi, where Bob O'Leary explains, "We are making a big push on digital, because we want to be the first global digital bank." He is a self-confessed convert who has made a point lately of immersing himself in this new world. He recently attended a master class called Hyper Island, a three-day plunge into digital for executives, and it got him fired up—and wired: "It changed my mindset from being a traditional marketer," he says. It taught him, "You have got to *live your life digital*. So I watch TV on my iPad now. I carry my iPad everywhere; all my meeting notes are on it. I pay all my bills online. Use GPS in the car. Everything I do is digital. It simplifies your life." O'Leary is a clear case of over-35 talent being brought happily into the digital world with a little effort and training. "It is the way of the future," he affirms. "It totally drives how you live professionally."

At Catholic University, Stewart McHie says today's companies "absolutely need people who are much more broadly educated, who understand the use of the new communication tools, the digital and mobile and social media, and the next-thing-that-if-I-knew-what-it-was-I-wouldn't-be-talking-to-you media." But part of the updated training, he stresses, needs to be about managing the flood of information that digital afflicts us with. The Internet, after all, has reached the stupendous size of five trillion megabytes. "No one is lacking for data! What is lacking is how to turn that into actionable steps," he argues. "We need to develop people who don't just produce 80-page PowerPoint presentations, but who can find the three or four nuggets that lead you to act. People who can boil down massive amounts of data and find important insights."

Leighanne Levensaler is vice president of application product management at Workday, a leading provider of enterprise cloud applications for human resources and finance, headquartered in Pleasanton, California. Speaking as an independent expert, she says she is convinced the new workforce will require constant retooling and recertification to stay current in all things digital: "We will all be in school forever. Instead of the rebirth of corporate universities, I believe we will see a rise in higher education institutions partnering with businesses to offer requalification in the sciences, engineering, and healthcare that are paid for or subsidized by the company."

Many companies are pushing hard for digital training throughout the organization, expanding IT know-how far beyond its original bounds. Mike Bailen outlined for me one such initiative at Zappos—z.code: "It is a six-week training program targeting individuals who have a strong interest in coding but do not necessarily have any formal experience or education. Zappos employees are encouraged to apply. Throughout the six weeks, the z.code students have the opportunity to learn about front-end and back-end web development. I am happy to say that a Customer

Loyalty Team representative [call center rep] was able to secure a position within our front-end development team after the program ended."

As Bailen suggests, expanding access to digital skills makes excellent sense given the acute shortage of tech talent today. "We wish we saw four times more digital e-commerce social marketing people," one recruiter recently lamented to me.

FOR DIGITAL INSIGHTS, LOOK OUTSIDE YOUR INDUSTRY

Even as you try to bring your staff up-to-date on the technology revolution, you may find yourself seeking further expertise from elsewhere—perhaps far afield. There is a definite trend of companies bringing in digital talent from outside their own industries. This really shakes up the talent game: How do you find, evaluate, and attract these people who are coming from highly unfamiliar settings?

Consider the airline industry. Mark Bergsrud first entered marketing in 2000; since then, he has seen dramatic change. By the time he left his position at United in 2013, he says, "The largest part by far of my 225-person marketing department was teams on e-commerce and merchandising, quality-control professionals for the website, translation and localization—it was all very IT focused. We still had advertising and product design and development, but all our growth was in e-commerce. What we found is that we needed far more of these e-commerce experts, not airline professionals."

As a result of this shift, the airlines, like other industries, are competing with entirely different industries for the same scarce talent. As Bergsrud explains, "Suddenly, we were in competition with other big companies for those employees. Traditionally, airlines had not paid high salaries in management because people were attracted to a business with sizzle and sex appeal, plus they loved the free-travel benefit. Nowadays, airline companies are in almost constant recruiting mode. They need to attract people with cool glasses and Mohawks and purple hair."

The automotive sector finds itself in a similar situation. According to Douglas Speck, senior vice president of marketing, sales, and customer service at Volvo Car Corporation, "One of the evolutions in the car business is the integration of digital into your experience of your automobile, a very intuitive use of your car. This is a new world for us: 'How do I connect my car to a cloud?' It requires a new understanding of the technology as well as the commercial potential." In response, they are hiring people from far outside the automotive field: "This week, I interviewed a woman from the video gaming industry."

It is difficult to find these digital experts, Speck says, especially when you are in an industry they do not connect with digital. "We are having a hard time attracting talent. Many potential recruits perceive themselves as being on the leading-edge of the world and wonder, 'Am I going to be bored there? It takes four to five years to bring a car to market. Will there be monolithic leadership in such an old-fashioned industry?' We hire them knowing they are going to leave us."

I also spoke with Paul Brown, former president of brands and commercial services at Hilton Worldwide, who told me, "We have no shortage of experienced talent in the hotel industry, but there is a shortage of next-generation talent, the kind that can help the industry innovate appropriately. The hotel business has been slow to change, in many ways." Who is this next-generation person they are looking for? "It is the individual who can bring in expertise from outside the industry but also find a way to get things done in this industry. That has proven quite difficult to find."

AMID HYPERCHANGE, EVERYONE NEEDS TO CONSTANTLY LEARN . . . AND RELEARN

Futurist Alvin Toffler once warned, "The illiterate of the twenty-first century will not be those who cannot read and write, but those who cannot learn, unlearn, and relearn." For the staunch traditionalist, this pronouncement was chilling, pointing to a world in which nothing would be definite or fixed or permanent, but instead where we will throw out our belief systems like a ketchup-stained McDonald's bag, only to acquire another one tomorrow.

And yet Toffler's future is here now. In our interview with John Sullivan at San Francisco State University, he constantly referred to VUCA—originally a military term—which stands for *volatility, uncertainty, complexity, ambiguity. Fast Company* magazine highlighted these very phenomena in describing "Generation Flux": "The vast bulk of our institutions—educational, corporate, political—are not built for flux. Few traditional career tactics train us for an era where the most important skill is the ability to acquire new skills."[1]

In today's Darwinian struggle to get ahead, when the business world is thoroughly shaped by VUCA, "It is all about being a learning human being," says Stephanie Tilenius, formerly of Google and eBay. "The people who are most aggressive about learning new skills and trying new things will be the most successful." Extending business management expert Tom Peters's notion of "The Brand Called You," Tilenius is clear that a relentless drive to learn is what talent now needs to succeed: "People need to be much more flexible, adaptable, more aggressive about learning new skills. Everyone needs to be an entrepreneur in his or her own career."

Joe Kennedy has a stellar track record of leading companies where learning has been a strategic must. He was part of the startup team at Saturn and then had a five-year stint as president and CEO of E-Loan before taking on those same positions at Pandora Media. "When I started back then, and in a more traditional industry, the skills you needed didn't change so fast. Now we live in a world of perpetual learning and re-learning. Back then, you could master a set of skills and they had a longer useful life. But then 15 years ago, suddenly you had to learn Java and the web. And then the smartphone revolution came along, with whole new languages and environments. The rate at which talent has to learn and adapt has accelerated." He talks encouragingly about today's conditions being a positive, humane evolution toward an environment in which people can work at their best, provided they are willing to learn: "If people come through their educational years without any embrace of the concept of learning, or having learned how to learn, that is a problem. Societally and culturally, we have to embrace the fact that learning is foundational."

Traditionalists may decry today's Toffler-like era of constant upheaval and intellectual reinvention, but Kennedy sees it as full of upsides: "People are challenged in today's world to continue to develop. That is a better and more natural place to be than in the very artificial world of the past, where you worked for a company for 35 years and left with a gold watch."

At The Weather Company, David Kenny similarly sees promise in all the turmoil. Digital is fast transforming his business—for example, allowing him to collate global forecasts: Because weather travels around the spinning globe, this makes the American forecast more accurate. Also they are learning to let machines make the predictions, "since humans make a forecast worse. But those humans are now free to do more original science. The same people have been working on getting the five-year forecast today as accurate as the three-day forecast was" some years ago. Far from losing out to a technology that rendered them superfluous, his employees have thrived under the new, tumultuous conditions.

DISPERSING DIGITAL KNOW-HOW

Recently, I found it highly encouraging when two of our employees at Havas Worldwide New York—director of user experience Bryan Keller and director of creative technology Eric Ackley—took it upon themselves to organize an after-hours "Think and Drink Meetup" a couple of times a month at local bars. These meetups are intended to bring others within the agency up to speed on what's happening in digital, with each session concentrated on a different topic. First up: "Designing Great Touch and Invisible Interfaces for the Mobile World." As Ackley explains, "We have a wealth of talent in the building and lots of interesting and important conversations going on. This is a great way to get some of those discussions happening with more people." He also intends to roll out a more formal class, which will center on hour-long deep dives into very specific topics. It's an outstanding example of how digital know-how can—and should—be spread across organizations.

HIRE FOR THE FUTURE, NOT THE PAST

Tomorrow has a way of creeping up on you. Will you recognize the next big thing when you see it? Will your employees?

I'm reminded of the story about IBM in the early days of the Internet. Someone reportedly asked at a senior management meeting what the Internet was all about, and the technical expert in the room dismissed it as nothing more than a way for academics to communicate with one another. So they all concluded that it had absolutely nothing to do with IBM.

Of course, none of us can see clearly into the future, but with the right mix of background and training, today's talent can do a much better job of anticipating what is possibly coming next and not dismiss a gigantic breakthrough as having nothing to do with their company, as IBM once did.

Paul Brown muses on the importance of hiring forward-looking talent, putting his finger on an unfortunate paradox: "Companies are looking for the future, but they hire on the past. And there will be a high likelihood of being disappointed. You want people to do things that are new, to change the organization, to 'make us better at this.' But then in interviewing people, what do they say?—'Tell me what you've done, give me four examples.' But if people are truly innovative, they probably have not done it yet." For Brown, hiring needs to focus not on past experiences so much as on capabilities. Tilenius agrees: "I think the whole notion of talent is changing. It is more about what you know, what skills you go acquire, and not just your resume."

THE GREAT DIGITAL DIVIDE FAVORS
FORWARD-THINKERS OVER FOSSILS

Every great transformation in human history—every great crisis—has propelled some people to success and fortune while burying others. The digital revolution is no exception. It has opened a gulf between employees who are capable of handling the new realities and those who are not.

Inevitably, a generational dimension appears. Shoulder-to-shoulder in offices across America are workers old enough to remember the first Apollo moon landing—which is said to have required all the computing power of a single Google search query today—and workers too young to clearly remember a planet without dot-coms, web surfing, or email. "We see a tremendous digital divide," says David Wilkie of World 50. With new hires, digital is "the way everything is," not some newfangled option. And as for the old-fashioned way of thinking, "They don't even understand that."

At the same time, the technology that younger workers so often delight in and that is infused throughout their entire lives leaves some older workers feeling insecure. I think a crisis has arisen around this issue— namely, the senior, highly experienced, and once-valuable employee who has become demoralized and disengaged, unable to make the transition to the digital future.

THE PROBLEM OF "THE FADING FIFTY"

Jerry Noonan, global consumer practice leader at executive-search consulting firm Spencer Stuart, muses about the frenetic rate of change, the quickening pace of business process and information flow, and the demand for new skills and mental agility. Even people with a successful track record are now struggling to keep up. Looking to the future, he expects continuing acceleration for the next generation of workers: "They will see two or three cycles of how business is done during the course of their careers." Employees with ingrained habits are clearly at risk, he argues.

When I look at how midlevel and senior executives are coping with the pace of change in business, I see what I would term the Forward versus the Fading Fifty. Though these people are in the same age cohort— ranging from, say, their late 40s through to retirement age—they are of vastly different mindsets. The Forward Fifty are active and engaged and relentlessly curious. The Fading Fifty are staid, talking about the past more than the future, signaling a greater interest in balance-in-life than in pushing themselves toward what's next.

In numerous conversations I have had with business leaders, the forlorn figure of the Fading Fifty has repeatedly shuffled onto the stage. Who are the Fading Fifty? They are workers who were respected 20 years ago but now are drifting to the sidelines in this new environment; they are no longer leading the charge. They are holding onto the older model of a senior, distant leadership role, guiding from afar, waiting for people to come to them. They have lost a sense of constant curiosity and lifetime learning.

For many members of the Fading Fifty, despondency begins to creep in because they feel they are not being honored for their hard-won experience. It is a paradoxical truth of our transformed age: Experience, once seemingly so priceless, can now be a liability if it has not been coupled with continuous relearning. Because who cares what a person accomplished way back in the 1990s, when few of today's conditions applied? Seriously, in 1997, there wasn't even a Google.

Havas Creative Group's chief digital officer, Matt Howell, recognizes how tough it can be when hard-won experience suddenly becomes irrelevant. "Some mindsets get embittered; they do not want to let go of things they know, and they become obstacles in the organization." As a recruiter with more than two decades of professional insights, Elizabeth Zea cautions that, for talent, experience can actually be a millstone if it is not constantly updated. Companies now want workers who are "more adaptable, more entrepreneurial, more digital." And too often they look askance at the Fading Fifty: "With age, the less adaptive you get, by nature. People have invested a lot of time to know something. So to reboot, it is scary."

If you are concerned about building effective teams—and this is more important now than ever—you have to worry about the inability of the Fading Fifty to work with millennials or the millennial-minded. Some workplace veterans may scoff at generation Y even as they have young people with tattoos and piercings in the corner doing their work for them.

Millennials quickly grow frustrated with having this kind of Luddite above them, says Wilkie, who describes "a chasm, a divide" between the two mentalities. It hurts companies, he argues, "when millennials think, 'All the people above me are dinosaurs.' So they jump ship. They just do not see their progression within the organization."

The Fading Fifty had better change their ways or the boom will fall on them. Matt Howell agrees, believing that companies will increasingly choose to eliminate the deadwood with outdated skills who are pulling in a big paycheck because of seniority but bring little actual value to the organization. "These people have lost the ability to contribute in other areas, and they are not worth the money. You don't want to pay for the parts you aren't using."

AND THE PROMISE OF THE FORWARD FIFTY

In contrast to the Fading Fifty are their future-focused, enthusiastic counterparts, the Forward Fifty. I am constantly impressed by the many people I meet who show all the creativity and curiosity of generation Y and yet are senior in their careers. A perfect case: One of my colleagues spent many years thinking in terms of 30-second TV spots. But he did not get stuck there when the world changed around him—far from it. Today he works comfortably in teams where everybody talks about in-store experience, leveraging data, and Facebook. He has made the transition. He is turned on by the new and the next.

Wilkie agrees: "You can be 58 or 65 and be the guru on digital customer support. There is no reason you cannot be as good, or better, than a younger person." Noonan concurs: "It is not age-specific. It is the adaptability, the individual's ability to grow and learn; it is desire and intellectual curiosity, not intelligence. Regardless of age, you will see people who are exploring versus people doing the same thing they have done for the past ten years. There is an intellectual agility that defines how people are going to keep up with the inevitable changes in business, this pace of change."

"Don't play defense," The Weather Company's David Kenny advises more experienced colleagues who are frightened of the future. Digital may replace you, yes, but "it frees up humans to be creative." Rather than being afraid of being pushed aside, these people should embrace the change because it is going to happen, and it will liberate them to do some more interesting work.

At this point, it might seem as though there is no upside to aging in a workplace that prizes the attributes of younger talent, but there is. Older workers can give themselves an edge by cultivating the virtues described throughout this book (digital, adaptive, learning) and by leveraging their life experiences into places of leadership. Matt Howell rates this as something older workers frequently do better: "I think their general leadership qualities—how to manage teams, how to deal with high-level client engagements—you find less frequently with younger folks." Elizabeth Zea offers a similarly encouraging counterblast to ageism: "You can make a senior leader more digital, but you cannot make a very digital junior person a leader."

And, of course, not all millennials are agile and adaptive in their thinking. In fact, according to Kris Szafranski at The Nerdery, they may actually be less adaptive than people who are older and more seasoned: "I would say that some of the younger employees are more resistant to change. Midcareer workers have gotten used to changing jobs and having ups and downs. But the young don't know what they don't know." They think things will always be the same as they are now.

CODA: DIGITAL ISN'T EVERYTHING

With all of today's obsession with the Internet and digital tools, more traditional concerns have often been forgotten. But let us not overlook the fact that there is much about life and business that has nothing to do with gigabytes. Many of us are now deliberately going off the grid from time to time in order to reestablish balance and reconnect with the older ways of thinking. At home, I have started powering down my iPhone. And in meetings, I pointedly turn it face down. I find that many others do the same so they can focus on real face time and old-school human interaction.

I talked with Michael Powell about these issues. "We are doing things at a relentless rate and confuse being busy with being productive," he feels. "I think how much time employees waste just deleting unnecessary emails! It adds up." He rejects the notion that millennials are the effortless master-multitaskers. "There is confusion between real work and accomplishment...and playing with your BlackBerry. People have this intense 'need to feel connected,' but their attention is divided. All these gadgets, and I ask, 'Who is the slave of whom?'" Powell believes it is essential for leaders to decide the ground rules for technology. He tells his employees, "Don't email me if you are within 30 feet of me. That's a rule."

He describes himself as a techno-evangelist who advocates a thorough level of digital literacy for all future talent, but he emphasizes that digital is a tool, not an end in itself: "I remind my employees: You are chasing knowledge and wisdom, not pushing data and information." He is emphatic that all reasonable people nowadays are going to have an ambivalent relationship with digital technology. "My computer may be an access portal to knowledge...it may be a tool...but my computer is not Descartes."

At the Aspen Institute, Eric Motley, managing director of the Henry Crown Fellowship program, similarly stresses that "to be an effective leader in a highly digital environment, you need to make room for individual dialogues, face-to-face. You need to look them in the eye and hold them accountable." The very fact that we have to remind ourselves to unplug occasionally is a testament to the phenomenal reach of the digital revolution. It will only grow and expand in years to come, we know, and so much of business success requires our grappling with it and with its radical implications for the nurturing of talent in a world in which, it seems, we live half our lives online.

This for me is critical and perhaps the greatest paradox of the digital revolution. We have never derived more value from being switched on, and yet we have never needed to switch off more. It is one of my greatest challenges. I make an extra effort to create time to be truly present, to engage in dialogues without multitasking. I think it is vital, both for me and for whomever I am interacting with.

QUESTIONS TO ASK YOURSELF

- What is your organization's relationship to the digital revolution? If you are constantly playing catch-up, what do you need to change to be a digital innovator?
- What are you doing to ensure the baby boomers within your company are as fluent in new technology as those digital natives, the millennials?
- What more can you do to incentivize perpetual learning and the addition of new skills? How can you make both of these things a standard part of the workplace rather than something that takes place in off-site locations and just a few days of the year?

STRATEGY FOUR

CREATE A SENSE OF DYNAMISM

CHAPTER 12

HIRE FOR AGILITY

I FIRST MET MICHELE BUCK, SENIOR VICE PRESIDENT AND chief growth officer at Hershey, four years ago. You can really see the difference that intelligent talent management makes by looking at Hershey. Although ancient by corporate standards (119 years old, whereas the average age of companies today stands at just 15 years), the business has never grown stale because it is perpetually innovative in its thinking and actions. It outperforms the competition year after year, not by rolling out new line extensions but by investing in and making smart use of talent.

Beyond Buck's sheer smarts, I have been impressed with her relentless quest for knowledge; it is what makes her insights so valuable. Her advice to companies that aspire to succeed in the manner Hershey has for so long:

1. *Seek agile people.* "In high-potential screening we are looking for strong thinkers who can apply that to different types of business problems. We identify them by how they do their jobs: They tend to focus first on the big picture and then on how their piece is going to contribute—How can they make a game-changing impact? They don't have the assumption that things are givens but instead step back and see the broader context."

2. *Make use of the matrix.* "With globalization, we are operating in matrix organizations, where you have to be able to work across. We move the best people into nontraditional assignments. We reserve global moves for folks who are the most talented and who thrive on learning; we not only move up those people, we give them a chance to really broaden."

3. *Have talent try on new roles.* In her career, Buck was broadened by taking on a highly novel challenge: managing a troubled manufacturing plant after she had been in marketing for years. Rather than let the plant muddle along and perhaps be shuttered, she fought to keep it open and devoted a week per month to being on-site, even laboring alongside the line workers. "It was a very impactful growth experience. It was an example of seizing an opportunity presented to you. I could have minimized the plant experience. It was risky, given I did not have deep background there. It expands your mind; you learn about working with people in different environments. It shaped me to look to the future and say, 'I'd love to take on new and different things.'" In an interview a number of years ago, Buck pointed to the relationships she built with those plant employees as the greatest reward of her career: "When I left, I received a plaque embroidered by the wife of a union employee in a frame made by the shop mechanics, reading: 'Our Loss Is Their Gain.'"[1]

To my mind, Michele Buck is a striking example of today's top talent: self-motivated, determined to forge connections, and, above all, agile. She does not stick to the well-trodden path; instead, she tries new things, regardless of the naysayers. This aptitude for serial adaptation will distinguish the strongest companies of tomorrow.

AGILITY MATTERS MORE NOW

"Because of the speed of change," says Carlos Abrams-Rivera at Mondelēz International, there is a higher premium than ever before on "flexibility and agility. In the past, we tended to look for mental horsepower and skill sets, but mental agility is something we now particularly value as the world gets smaller every day. I am glad to hire people who are smart, but I am more glad to hire people who are agile and flexible."

David Ulrich of the University of Michigan provides a useful framework for a discussion of the new talent mandate by listing four criteria he recommends companies use to identify high-potential talent: ambition, ability, agility, and achievement. And in a report written with his research partner Norm Smallwood, Ulrich describes the four types of agility they found to be most vital:

- Learning agility: curious, finds simplicity in complexity, identifies quick rules of thumb
- People agility: self-aware, committed to personal growth, works to help others succeed
- Change agility: likes to tinker and experiment, tries new things, accepts failure
- Results agility: flexible in ideas, good in new situations, works well with teams[2]

Not everyone you hire will excel equally in all four measures of agility, but top performers will display all of these to an above-average degree. Take a closer look at this list, and I think you will see that each one represents traits that have grown significantly more valuable to your organization over the last decade or two.

Agility is closely allied with what Stanford psychologist Carol Dweck calls a "growth mindset." Those who believe in a "fixed mindset" consider a person's intelligence and innate talent as static and therefore little able to be improved through effort or training. Those with a growth mindset, in contrast, believe that brains and natural aptitudes are merely a starting point, and that a person's accomplishments owe less to his or her innate abilities than to what the person does to use and strengthen those abilities. Surely, the most successful companies of today and tomorrow will embrace the growth point of view, always promoting learning, always pushing to accomplish more with what they have and what they can get.

Sometimes the people most resistant to growth are the talent themselves. That has to change, says Cindi Cooper, who as Gap International's co-chief operating officer is responsible for the global growth and expansion of the company:

> *Everybody says, "You've got to hire the right talent" but that is only part of the picture. If those people are not organized to grow in their capacities—in their leadership and expertise capacities—it is talent with limits. Too often, people have certain assumptions of what they are capable of; they say they are a certain way. "I am a marketing guru," for example, and they don't think they can be anything else. So everybody ends up in some kind of box. But we ask them, "Could you move out of marketing into R&D? From sales to manufacturing?" We open up the assumptions set. Because all those fixed assumptions actually keep the system stuck. People grow weeds around them. You don't get the new growth, and you don't get the energy of growth, which is huge for talent retention. We believe that people can go way beyond what they think they are capable of.*

DRIVEN BY DOWNSIZING

You do not have to look back far to see what is driving the push for more agile workers. Tough economic conditions after 2007 forced us all to focus on people with the aptitude—and attitude—to cope with unsettled conditions. "If you can't adjust to changing times, you'll be left behind," Citi's Bob O'Leary cautions. "That is just how it is. Everything has to be more efficient and effective. Budgets are cut all the time. We are looking for ways to reduce the complexity in the way we work in the organization, making things simpler."

I have certainly seen this in my own industry, as budgets have compressed and anyone deemed less than essential has been cut from the roster.

Truth be told, it would be hard to find an industry in which payrolls were not winnowed during the Great Recession.

As job after job has vanished, some specialized tasks have disappeared, but the bulk of the tasks have been thrown onto the rest of us. Today we all have to juggle many more roles than previous executives would have considered possible. That has led marketer Mark Bergsrud to conclude that there is a much-reduced role for the merely ordinary worker as opposed to the superstar: "Merely average performance is not good enough anymore. With small staffs you need above average." He has seen entire categories of jobs disappear. "We hardly have any executive assistants anymore. I book my own travel and handle many other tasks that previously would have been done by an assistant. Everybody has got to have a broader skill set. If you are in advertising, you must do your own financial and budget work. We need very well rounded people when we are smaller. People need more skill."

And guess what? We will continue to be expected—and expect those in our employ—to take on even more roles. Currently, a lot of us are adding social media skills and figuring out how to do things like crowdsource or even crowdfund. Who knows what will be considered essential next? What it all adds up to is that each of us has to be a turnkey worker, capable of operating without the assistance of all those specialized employees who once formed the underpinnings of the company. All of us have to be constantly learning, adding skills, and willing to take on new tasks.

FIGURING IT OUT AND GETTING IT DONE

A great part of the value of the agile worker lies in what he or she can accomplish without any help. Dan Clifford is cofounder and chief experience officer at AnswerLab, a top user-experience research and testing firm headquartered in San Francisco. His firm provides extensive training, yet candidates who are hired are expected to have the agility to seek answers on their own when needed rather than always relying on others to bring them up to speed. "One of our core values is, 'Figure it out and get it done,'" he says. "It's important—it reflects a level of flexibility and resourcefulness. And it is only going to be more important as companies reorganize and technology changes. Teams have got to be flexible and be able to drive change with less top-down direction."

Citi's O'Leary subscribes to a philosophy of "agility over strategy." With the banking industry in rocky times, he told us, "We are looking for a person who sees the current challenges as an opportunity. People need to work amid ambiguity, to be adaptive and agile. If you can find the right people, they will want to stay and roll up their sleeves. They will want to be part of the turnaround."

MINDS WIDE OPEN

As the world becomes increasingly diverse and global, adaptiveness must also include the ability to converse and work effectively with co-workers, clients, and others from a wide range of backgrounds. Old silos have crumbled. It is more important than ever before to have talent who can fit in anywhere and work with anyone, regardless of background, field, or even personality. At Vorbeck Materials, John Lettow describes the altered terrain of today's more diverse workplace: "One thing we have tried to do is to establish a pretty open culture. A person interviewing here once asked me, 'What does it take to fit in around here?' I had to think about that a little bit. And the answer is flexibility. We have a lot of different personalities, and most people are not ashamed to express their personality and views. If you are too set or rigid, it would be difficult for you here. Hopefully, this keeps us open and respectful; open to a wide range of employees who would be comfortable here. So that we have a broader pool to pick from."

To some extent, this goes back to the point I made about not hiring jerks. But it is really more than that: I place a premium on people whose first impulse is not to reject or disagree with alternative viewpoints but to give careful consideration to their validity—and maybe even learn something from the experience. This does not mean I am looking for a conflict-free workplace. A bit of friction can electrify the creative process. But I no longer have much patience for small-minded types whose myopia puts up needless barriers.

IN SEARCH OF HYBRIDS

The notion of the hybrid worker goes hand in hand with discussions of agility, for hybrids are capable of adapting their skill sets and methods as needed. In the old way of working, it made sense to hire specialists who would perform the same tasks over and over, all the way up to retirement. But that is no longer applicable in most businesses, where skill sets need to evolve constantly and where many current functions are likely to be extinct in the future. We all need people who are sufficiently agile to combine disparate skills and specializations with an intense curiosity and immense capacity for growth. More and more, we need people who combine specific attributes best suited to the business.

What I have found in talking with business leaders is that the hybridization they seek is no longer necessarily linked just to skills but also to innate aptitudes. So while a company may be looking for someone who has earned both an MBA and a JD, what really matters may be less the combined learning than the medley of useful traits such a person is likely to bring to the group. Mike Abbott at Kleiner Perkins Caufield & Byers says that what he seeks in a new recruit is "not really skills. It is very high IQ and a very high EQ (emotional quotient). I look for both of those things together. Because, even if they are really junior, they will have the ability to become leaders. Also, are they intellectually curious?"

At FieldView Solutions, developer of software for managing the infrastructure of very large data centers, Sev Onyshkevych says he looks for a combination of breadth and depth: "Everybody needs a combination of both—people who can see the big picture, yet are focused and get it done." In hiring, he avoids anyone who seems to have tunnel vision, who has done only one thing their whole career or is the world's biggest expert on a single, narrow topic. "In entrepreneurship," he says, "this is fundamental." Heineken's Dolf van den Brink agrees, but he rejects the notion of hiring hybrids *or* specialists. He wants both: "There has been a great deepening of functional expertise, and if you are not mastering it, you are in trouble, because of competition for jobs. When I am hiring, I want the deepest skills and competence in each area. And yet in this hyperinnovative and hyperdynamic environment, where tomorrow will be entirely different from today, you need people who see the big picture."

With everything morphing before our eyes, I agree we need hybrids and specialists, but I tend to stack my teams with the former. In my experience, these are the types most likely to be capable of visionary insights, which are what every company needs right now amid cloudy and confusing storm fronts of change.

T-SHAPED TALENT AND A T-SHAPED TEAM

The adaptive employee will be, ideally, of the much-lauded T shape, broadly experienced yet with one deep specialization or "spike." That is just the sort of worker Mike Bailen says Zappos is looking for: "We need our employees to be versatile and adaptable because Zappos embraces and drives change (this is a core value, after all). If employees are too specialized and compartmentalized, it limits our ability to evolve. However, we do need our new hires to fully understand and deliver on the job they are brought in for."

Elizabeth Zea and her partner in their executive recruiting agency relay that their clients all seem to want the same thing: adaptive and flexible senior executives. "The senior person that is a mile deep and an inch wide is less relevant today," she told me. "It has gotten to the point where we will only recruit senior people with hybrid skill sets, talent with two or three different skill-set experiences. "For example, a general marketer with a digital spike. That's different—companies are no longer purist in what they are seeking."

Even with the spike, the critical attribute is always adaptiveness. As her agency recruits top talent for many companies, "We are only interested in hybrids. Unless you are hybrid—unless you come to the party with a wide vantage point and flexibility and are adaptive, you are not going to be successful."

THE VALUE OF THE LIBERAL ARTS MAJOR

I graduated from Georgetown University with a BFA in 1993, so I am pleased to see that the liberal arts degree has not been written off entirely in this high-tech world. On the contrary, after two decades of heavy emphasis on hiring graduates with specific technical and digital skills, businesses are turning once again to liberal arts majors, whom I consider uniquely positioned to fill roles that require a holistic, agile mindset.

Universities are recognizing the trend and at the same time are making changes to adapt their offerings to the changing landscape. At Georgetown, where I serve on the College Board of Advisors, an undergraduate can now major in English and minor (for the first time) in business. So even the most traditional liberal arts institutions are recognizing the value of a hybrid approach.

Stewart McHie directs a master's program in business for nonbusiness majors at Catholic University. "What we find from a talent standpoint is that CEOs like the combination a lot," he says, "because business students are not broadly enough educated; they need more of the liberal arts. They are very narrowly focused, and their education has been pointed toward skill sets. Instead, they need history, philosophy. Employers like critical-thinking skills from a liberal arts background. These students have read more, written more in their disciplines. Writing skills are really lacking in many businesses."

Liberal arts majors are similarly appealing to Belinda Lang, who most recently was head of brand, digital, and consumer marketing at Aetna: "Early career people need to be flexible and adaptable because priorities are changing very quickly. We need cross-functional thinking. It is not just enough to know your narrow function." Also wanted: "People who can write, think, and follow up, and are willing to learn."

Lang cites the success of two recent hires: "One a religious studies major, the other an English major. They could write well and think critically; they were not afraid to ask questions and speak to people. They came in with intellectual curiosity and an eagerness to learn. This kind of nontraditional person does very well in business."

I met cable and telecom executive Michael K. Powell through the Aspen Institute, where he sits on the board of trustees. Powell, who graduated from the College of William and Mary with a degree in government and earned his JD from Georgetown University Law Center, stresses the value of liberal arts training in producing the sorts of hybrids he is looking to hire. He offered this example:

> *My 18-year-old son is in computer science at the University of Texas in Austin. Loves computers. He asked me the first semester, "Dad, why do I have to take this sociology class? Why can't I just take computer classes?" And I said, "Do you think Mark Zuckerberg is a computer scientist or a sociologist? What problem did he solve? Facebook is really an understanding of social interactions. Zuckerberg was a nerdy kid unhappy with the social dynamic on campus. There is nothing technologically fancy about Facebook! In that sociology class, you might hear something that leads you to found the next multibillion-dollar company. Likewise, Steve Jobs was not a great technician; he knew enough to be conversant in his language, but he had the creative spirit and a maniacal commitment to persevere. His emotional quotient . . . and being creative about the connection with the human spirit . . . these made him better than HP."*

All this adds up to a critical need for people who have the flexibility to adapt along with the company, people who can come up with fresh visions and pathways for the organization—and for themselves. In the next chapter, we look at what smart companies are doing to promote adaptiveness in their ranks.

QUESTIONS TO ASK YOURSELF

- What are the three most important things you could be doing to better promote agility in your workforce?
- What emerging skills will your talent of tomorrow need to master? And what more should you be doing to help your people learn these skills today?
- Is it time to change up the pathways through which you seek fresh talent? Where are the people with the combination of skills you need most apt to be?

CHAPTER 13

MOVE PEOPLE AROUND

ONCE YOU HAVE BROUGHT ON BOARD HIGHLY AGILE talent, you need to do all you can to keep their curiosity roiling and their skill sets growing. The best way to do that is by never letting them stay in one place for too long—not physically and in most cases not functionally. In the old way of running an organization, talent flowed in one of two directions: up or out. Career paths were pretty much standardized, and most people had a fairly good sense of how their careers would plot out. But today, the timeworn ladder of career progress is morphing into a more flexible lattice or matrix, with talent scuttling in all sorts of directions and along some unexpected paths.

A number of factors are at work here, and they are not all related to carefully planned schemes to keep workforces agile. David Wilkie of World 50 points to the lack of expansion among most U.S. businesses as a key driver. "Companies must do more lateral transfers," he says, "because there is slow market growth, and that means fewer rising tides for everyone. Because companies are not growing and creating jobs, the people above you are not moving out of your way."

Globalism is largely responsible for the new matrix pattern in career paths at Edelman, the world's largest public relations firm. Employees have been encouraged since 2010 to move geographically to gain a global perspective, reports chief talent officer Claudia Patton: "It is not the traditional ladder. It can be a jungle gym: You can move sideways, like a lattice." At Intel, workers shift into new positions every 18 to 24 months, and new hires are told, "Welcome to your next five jobs."

Just because the ladder-to-lattice transition is becoming more standard does not mean, of course, that everyone is finding it easy. At fast-growing Rackspace, which is transforming into a software company as the cloud-computing revolution unfolds, Henry Sauer says, "We need people to jump into roles they might not be ready for." Managers are on the lookout for promising talent, and they constantly provide feedback. But some newcomers "struggle, coming from a more structured environment with really well-defined career paths. It is more a zigzag here."

THE MANY ADVANTAGES TO FREQUENT MOVES

Regardless of which factors are spurring this less linear approach to career progression—or whether every individual is quite ready for it—this shift is a good thing for organizations. There are a number of distinct advantages to shaking things up from time to time.

One big plus to today's matrixes may be the demise of the Peter Principle, first identified in the 1960s, by which employees are, seemingly inevitably, promoted directly up the ladder until they come to rest on a rung that is too high for their innate abilities. They have, as the expression goes, "risen to their level of *in*competence." Lateral shifts might just solve this time-honored problem.

Another advantage to shuffling employees around is that such moves frequently suit them from a psychological perspective. The Weather Company CEO David Kenny told me, "The talent challenge is, if people are ambitious and want to win in a knowledge economy, they are always looking for new challenges every 18 months. So you must rotate them. It's your own darn fault if they leave you, otherwise."

Millennials, especially, seem to thrive on frequent change. "This generation views itself as more mobile and less committal," says Spencer Stuart's Jerry Noonan. "Young people all assume they are going to be moving to new employers, and companies are recognizing that moving these workers around to new positions and fresh challenges can help keep them happy longer." Lateral challenges offer good opportunities for "restless individuals still in a young, very curious stage in their lives. You shouldn't force them to do something narrow. You want to create a stimulating environment."

Moves can be physical or virtual. At Havas Worldwide, we have put in place an organized program that allows talent to work on a variety of projects, in different areas around the world. While in its infancy, we are already seeing success. People who go through our "movers" program develop skills and transferable experiences that they may not have been afforded in their home markets.

Regular changes in job responsibilities can also help to address employee burnout, a problem that has grown more acute as we expect fewer workers to handle more responsibilities. *Fast Company* quoted Steve McClatchy, founder of Alleer Training and Consulting, on the subject of movement on the job: "McClatchy believes happy employees don't stay in one role for too long. 'When there is movement in your life, there is satisfaction. Status quo is what creates burnout and ruts.' He says at companies such as Pfizer, staff achieves a balance between improvement, growth, and maintenance. Work burnout isn't about too many hours spent on the job, he contends, it's about feelings that come from improvement, or lack thereof."[1]

At The Nerdery, ample face time around the office allows managers to watch for changes in employees, according to Kris Szafranski: "What is their passion shifting to? Managers watch for this, continuing to get to know the person." The key to retaining good people, he says, is making sure you give them work that fits their personal abilities and goals as these change over time. "If we're not thinking like that, we're just relying on them to churn out code."

DESIGNING THEIR OWN PATHS AT THE MOTLEY FOOL

Moving your workers around can head off burnout and boredom, but, more compellingly, it can energize them tremendously. The Motley Fool encourages lots of movement, letting people constantly try new roles and create their own progressions. Recruiter Anessa Fike told me she had held three jobs at the company in the past two and a half years, which is typical of how they let people wear many hats.

One Fool cheerfully drives 90 minutes each way to work because he loves it there so much. He has held eight jobs in eight departments in nine years, Fike says, "because he wanted to really get in and learn about all these aspects of our company." By moving folks around, the organization has discovered skill sets they did not know employees had. "People have made their own jobs, new positions. You can create your own organic path to wherever you want to go. We help you write your own path." For example, an employee came forward from a tech area and said he had discovered a personal passion for health and wanted to be the in-house Wellness Fool. Now he does exactly that, having morphed into a full-time fitness and exercise specialist.

Matching personal interests with professional duties is something we practice at Havas Worldwide as well. Because we operate in almost every category of consumerism, we have a good deal of leeway to match people's skills, ambitions, and passions. One of the ways we have facilitated this is by creating a searchable talent database that has pulldowns on not just our people's professional achievements but also their personal passions. So we know who is obsessed with fashion, who has a strong interest in cars, and so on. This information is incredibly useful not just when we are looking to move people around but in undertakings such as new business pitches. We are able to create affinity teams around areas of passion that can hit the ground running or that we can plug into for counsel and expertise.

ENCOURAGING RISK-TAKING

Frequent moves do not just alter the fabric of the organization; they can also make lasting impressions on the individuals involved. Carlos

Abrams-Rivera of Mondelēz International is a strong believer in making moves, even when they are difficult. Jumping into a new position can be frightening, he admits: "I have been through many big challenges, things that looked pretty dark at the time. But now, I actually embrace those, because those are the moments you can learn the most from. You should change fear into an embracing of those opportunities. Because once you come out, you will be a better person and leader, even if you do not succeed. You should look for those opportunities where you are not comfortable, even if that means your career does not follow a straight path." He gives an example from his own experience. He was running part of Kraft when he was invited, over lunch, to take on a different assignment, far removed from his expected career trajectory. "I said sure. And in two weeks, I was walking the Great Wall of China—doing global marketing. I spent two years traveling 75 percent of the time, to Brazil, China, Russia—it was not a safe bet by any means," but it was highly valuable to him as an experience.

It is tremendously beneficial for organizations to give employees chances, big or little, to broaden themselves, he argues. "In the future, that is what will separate companies—which ones will allow those kinds of opportunities? Millennials are not going to learn from doing the same thing over time. Companies must allow employees to not just use their specialty strength but put them in a position to have a general view of the business."

BUILDING MORE HOLISTIC PERSPECTIVES

Abrams-Rivera makes an excellent point about gaining that general view. One of the chief advantages of moving employees around is that they get to see the whole company for the first time. John Costello, president of global marketing and innovation at Dunkin' Brands, Inc., shares that mindset: "At Dunkin', all our developmental and educational programs are geared to responding to a changing workplace," he says. "Today's business environment requires more agility and more cross-functional collaboration. Managers need to learn different skills and gain an appreciation of what other people do all day. They have to have better awareness of not only their own jobs but the world around them."

SAY GOODBYE TODAY, SAY HELLO TOMORROW

Part of the new flexibility that is so vital to modern businesses is coming to grips with the propensity of workers to jump not just from position to position but from company to company. Too often, businesses hyperventilate about their retention rate—it is a major preoccupation in my own industry, marketing communications—but retention percentages are ultimately just an arbitrary number. Eighty-five percent—is that good? And why, exactly? I would prefer employees leave if they are not a good fit here or if they feel a call to pursue some other avenue through which they will grow and gain skills. I would rather have an engaged workforce than a retained one. And I agree wholeheartedly with Walt Freese, who recalls, "At Ben & Jerry's, if somebody was ready for promotion after three to five years and we had no position for them, we would celebrate their going somewhere else—because we owed that to them in the [social] contract."

I am often asked how I handle it when people come and tell me they are leaving. My answer is simple: I am honest with them. If it is a great opportunity for them and they will develop further, I encourage them to do it. If not, I try to understand their motivations.

Joe Kennedy of Pandora Internet Radio understands the problem we all face with employees frequently switching jobs, and he shares my glass-half-full assessment: "We have far greater mobility of talent today than when I started my career," he told me. "People are no longer starting at a company and then spending decades there. Now, it's a string of experiences. And that intersects with the need to learn and relearn; they match up in an interesting way." As for staff jumping ship, "I don't view it entirely as a problem. I have learned to embrace the fact that an employee's career is not bounded by the concept, 'You only work in one place.' We want great people to stay here as long as it is a mutual win. But in some cases, the right thing for an employee to do is to move into another situation. And talent is also flowing in as it is flowing out. Our goal is not to have no turnover."

Recognizing that it is customary for people to shift employers frequently nowadays, I try to emphasize the quality of their exit. If you set the right tone in saying goodbye today, you may find yourself saying hello to the same talent at some point down the road, welcoming them back to your fold—but in the next go-around, they will bring enhanced abilities and experience.

Some advanced companies are taking specific steps to improve upon this goodbye–hello phenomenon. Cisco's Off/On Ramp program allows eligible employees to take a career break for up to two years, so long as they secure an open position in the firm before the end of their leave. Participating employees remain eligible for company-paid benefits during the first year.[2]

At global management-consulting firm McKinsey & Company, the culture includes attracting and developing exceptional people, who progress to become partners at McKinsey or go on to achieve distinction as leaders in the public, private, or social sector. One such person is Michael Zea, who spent seven years as a partner at McKinsey before becoming president and chief executive officer for the U.S. region at Aimia. When he left McKinsey, he recalls, "Many partners called and said, 'This is so cool, you're going to be a CEO. Can we sit down and get your input on what it was like at McKinsey and how we could serve our clients better?'" This kind of thoughtful approach is typical there, Zea says. "McKinsey stays in touch with people who have left; it's a very personalized and talent-focused approach."

Amazon CEO Jeff Bezos takes a particularly innovative—and generous—approach to helping workers make a positive exit:

> *Many of our fulfillment center employees will choose to build their careers at Amazon. For others, a job at Amazon might be a step towards a career in another field. We want to make it easier for employees to make that choice and pursue their aspirations.... So, for people who've been with us as*

little as three years, we're offering to pre-pay 95 percent of the cost of courses such as aircraft mechanics, computer-aided design, machine tool technologies, medical lab technologies, nursing, and many other fields. The program is unusual. Unlike traditional tuition reimbursement programs, we exclusively fund education only in areas that are well-paying and in high demand according to sources like the U.S. Bureau of Labor Statistics, and we fund those areas regardless of whether those skills are relevant to a career at Amazon.[3]

Now that is a remarkably creative and people-centric program. Also worthy of note is the fact that I first spotted that policy in an open letter Bezos shared with customers on Amazon's home page last summer. An effective way to remind customers of the people behind the brand.

As we have seen in this chapter, the premium today is very much on adaptability and getting the most out of the people on your payroll. In the next chapter, I address how smart companies are giving talent the freedom they need to excel.

QUESTIONS TO ASK YOURSELF

- What programs and policies have you put into place to ensure people are gaining the breadth of knowledge and experience they need to contribute fully to the company's growth?
- How are you ensuring that everyone has a variety of potential paths rather than being pigeonholed into one location or specialization?
- What are you doing to build positive and ongoing relationships with people who have chosen to leave the organization?

STRATEGY FIVE

BE PEOPLE-CENTRIC

CHAPTER 14

LOOSEN UP

Everything is about talent now. The older way in recruiting was, you hired a person and expected them to do it "our way." The new way is: Identify the talent and find out, how do they want to work?

—*John Sculley*

WE STAY IN TOUCH WITH FRIENDS AND ACQUAINtances via Facebook. We store our documents, music, and movies in the cloud. And we shop through our smartphones. So why is it that so many companies continue to try to keep their talent strapped to their physical desks of wood and metal? And why are so many employers refusing to forgo the old, rigid rules of the workplace that say workers need to be clocked in between certain hours on set days... or else?

Every business is different and has a unique set of needs. Some—such as brick-and-mortar retailers and manufacturing plants—absolutely need their laborers on-site and always there during specific hours. Many other businesses, however, have a wide swath of job functions that do not necessarily require that a person's duties be fulfilled in a set location and during a set time. The question is, then, are we sticking to the old way of doing things because we do not trust the talent we hire... or simply because we are stuck in the rut of doing things the way they have always been done?

Forward-thinking companies are reaping the benefits of people-centered policies that emphasize flexibility and individualization. My advice to you:

- Move to a results-based system.
- Be open to the zero-mile commute.
- Be flexible about job parameters.
- Support life-work integration.
- Insist on downtime.

MOVE TO A RESULTS-BASED SYSTEM

How much time is squandered in your workplace? What percentage of your talent have clocked out mentally even while their timesheets say they are clocked in? And how many would jump at the chance to have more control over their work environments—to be able to choose when and where they get their jobs done?

It seems Best Buy had the same questions. As an experiment, it launched the Results-Only Work Environment program, under which employees in participating departments were allowed to work virtually anywhere, anytime, so long as they successfully completed their assignments on time. The result: Productivity jumped 41 percent at headquarters; turnover dropped 90 percent.[1]

It is such a smart approach. When you think about it, why would we measure an individual's productivity in terms of the sheer number of hours he or she puts in at the office? That's nonsensical. It makes much more sense to measure everyone's value by what he or she produces, regardless of whether the work takes ten days, two days, or three hours. I am a big believer in results, and I also believe that you cannot overmanage your way there. At Havas Worldwide, we have put in place talent-assessment programs that place a higher premium on delivery than on anything else. In fact, as mentioned earlier, one of our favorite internal dicta is "spend more time doing and less time managing." That is not to say we want a workforce of totally independent operators. We just want people to know we measure our talent's value by what they produce, not by how long they spend hanging around the office.

At Palo Alto Software, Sabrina Parsons is clear about her preference for a results-based system: "Instead of, 'Where were you at 3 p.m. yesterday afternoon?' you should be saying, 'Wow, you got this in before time and the results are great.' Every time we meet, we stress that we manage in a results-oriented way. It is not, 'How long have you been here today?' but 'Why haven't you done these three things?' We are metrics driven, using data to make decisions and show results." Parsons especially cautions against employees staying too many hours at work just to make a big show of being there. "If you are waiting around the office until 8 p.m., and it is all about face time, tomorrow morning you won't want to be here. I worked in crazy startups with meetings at two in the morning, and people getting burned out—and they were only there for the face time."

As more businesses shake free of the old rules, we will see much more flexibility in the workplace, along with the emergence of new policies that take better account of individual circumstances and preferences. I see a clear sign of this trend in the results of the survey we conducted for this book: 86 percent of top executives agree that "the most successful companies are flexible and open to meeting employees' varied needs."[2]

> **Eighty-six percent of senior business leaders surveyed agree: "The most successful companies are flexible and open to meeting employees' varied needs."**

BE OPEN TO THE ZERO-MILE COMMUTE

A media hubbub occurred in early 2013 when Marissa Mayer banned telecommuting at Yahoo—a move that met with widespread criticism. I think she is swimming against a powerful trend that will only continue to strengthen as technologies improve and businesses discover the advantages of managing according to results rather than outmoded rules.

Already, according to a Reuters poll, about one in five workers around the globe—with heavy concentrations in the Middle East, Latin America, and Asia—telecommute frequently, and nearly 10 percent work from home daily.[3] In one U.S. example, Cisco has instituted Cisco Virtual Office, Cisco TelePresence, and Cisco WebEx, all to facilitate remote working and flexible work practices. Telecommuting is the rule, at least occasionally, for 90 percent of the company's employees.[4]

My goal is to hire people who will deliver, regardless of the circumstances. And I usually find that I don't need to place ironclad restrictions on them. I say, "Don't feel you need to come tell me that you are working from home today—it's OK. Now, it would not be OK for most people to do it five days a week, but you should absolutely do it when you need to." For your top talent, flexibility is an absolutely essential offering. You have to provide this if you do not want to lose really good people over piddling issues concerning scheduling.

A huge advantage in allowing workers flexibility is that you can avail yourself of the very best talent out there. In certain industries and job functions, it may not be necessary to visit headquarters at all. In a blog post, 37signals partner David Heinemeier Hansson summed it up well:

> *Every day I read a new article about some company whining about how hard it is to hire technical staff. Invariably it turns out that they're only looking for people within a commuter's distance of their office. I refuse to feel sorry for such companies. If we were only trying to hire in Chicago, we'd never have the world-class team we have today. . . . There's so much untapped tech talent that does not live near your office, but would work for you if you allowed them to. So stop whining, spend a day to get up to speed on remote working practices, and hire outside of your commuter zone.[5]*

BE FLEXIBLE ABOUT JOB PARAMETERS

Giving your talent the freedom to work remotely is a start, but for many employees, a matter of even greater importance is *when* they work. And, for some, that also means wanting more control over the number of hours a week they spend doing their jobs. All too often, some truly talented people are excluded from consideration for a job simply because they are unable to commit to the standard 40-hour workweek.

Flexible labor models that encourage individualization and a better balance are on the rise everywhere, says Workday's Leighanne Levensaler. These models may take a number of forms, including consulting jobs, temporary assignments, job sharing, and project-based work. They hold particular appeal for specific demographics: "There are more women in the workforce and in growing leadership roles. Flexible labor models and working arrangements can support families and the expectations of millennials," Levensaler points out.

A growing number of businesses seek to lure just these types of workers. According to Elizabeth Zea at JUEL Consulting, many of her client companies are trying to make themselves more attractive to working moms "who need life control." If you give them flexibility, along with meaningful work, she says, "They will do anything for you."

For Zea, several cohorts of workers are currently neglected in our thinking about talent. All could successfully be lured with an increased emphasis on balance. Case in point: the "dismissed older workforce. Ageism is alive and well in the marketing sector, for example. But these people have incredible value. Some have been displaced through no fault of their own, but because everybody wants the rising star, the person who is progressive and who 'looks of-today.'" The adaptive culture of the future, she predicts, will have "even more technology for enhanced remote communication. More virtual working, but finding the right people for that. More openness to flextime. Redefining what the workday is. You work forty hours, but maybe five of them are on Saturday."

SUPPORT LIFE-WORK INTEGRATION

In recent years, we have heard a good deal about life-work balance, which is not at all surprising given how work has managed to infiltrate just about every waking hour of our lives. We all know how difficult it is to break away, to put down the mobile device and stop checking texts and emails. I spoke with a colleague just this week who told me that her brother had chosen to spend his vacation at an ashram, not for religious or spiritual reasons, but because it was the one place he could think to go that would entirely prevent him from accessing the Internet.

I have long respected Yvon Chouinard as a pioneer in corporate social responsibility and workplace practices. It is telling that this founder of the Patagonia outdoors gear and apparel company chose to title his memoir *Let My People Go Surfing*. This title speaks perfectly to Chouinard's insistence that his employees continue to *live* even as they work. In naming Patagonia one of the Best Places to Work in 2011, *Outside* magazine cited the company's emphasis on a healthy integration of life and work:

> *It is culturally accepted for employees to take time off during their workday to pursue that balance, whether it is taking time off to spend time with their children, go surfing, skiing, or fly-fishing, or participate in one of the company's on-site sponsored exercise classes (free to employees). We trust employees to figure out a schedule that allows them to get their jobs done and also take care of themselves and their families.[6]*

Kelli Richards is CEO of The All Access Group—a digital music and entertainment consultancy—and a sought-after life coach in Silicon Valley. She remembers what it was like during the ten exciting but exhausting years she spent working for Apple, starting in 1987: "We wore T-shirts that said, 'Ninety Hour Work Weeks and Loving It,' but we weren't loving it. There were suicides and divorces. I always railed against that. Even now, I don't work on weekends, and I keep my evenings free."

Achieving this sort of balance is not easy. In our always-on, always-on-demand world, you need to be relentless about creating the space and the boundaries—and what suits one person may not work for another. I fight this battle with myself all the time. I have to make a conscious effort to put the iPhone down when I get home so I can tune in life and tune out work. Granted, I always end the evening by going back online and catching up, but that is after my older boys are asleep. I haven't entirely mastered the art of work containment, but I have found that recognizing the tendency to let my work invade personal time is critical to beginning to make a change.

With her highly successful clients, Richards says, "The most common issue is work-life balance. I tell them, 'You should live your passion.'" They are excelling in their careers, but, Richards warns them, "You still need to manage your life."

She notes a trend: "Increasingly, people want to liberate themselves from corporations and thrive as an expert under their own auspices." I told her that many companies I have spoken to seem worried about this shift. "Good!" she instantly replies. "More and more people are taking their expertise and leaving, and they are being more fulfilled. Corporations need to make people feel they are wanted and needed, not being overworked; that their lives are being prioritized, that they are being honored and motivated in personal ways."

Toy companies Mattel and Hasbro are headquartered on opposite coasts, but they share an approach to helping their talent lead more balanced lives. Both companies have half-day Fridays—year-round.[7]

INSIST ON DOWNTIME

If you are not focusing on work-life balance right now, what is that inattention doing to your employees? Without exception, the CEOs I spoke with seemed more worried about burnout among overzealous talent than about the occasional slacker. Boston Consulting Group has taken to issuing "Red Zone reports" when individuals are piling on too many hours week after week. When the situation is deemed sufficiently serious, the firm attempts to ameliorate it by extending the project timeline, bringing in more resources, or helping the consultant better budget his or her time.[8]

Burnout is a pressing problem that will only get worse as we find more seamless ways to work from anywhere, anytime. In numerous conversations across all kinds of sectors, I heard expressions of concern:

- "We are very conscious of it," says Dunkin' Brands' John Costello. "We encourage vacations and don't expect immediate responses while on vacation. We have flexible hours. We work hard to respect personal life."
- "I don't like people working on the weekends," Quixey's Tomer Kagan told us. "When you get burnout, work quality drops. I will sometimes come by on the weekends and kick people out."
- In the field of animal protection, dedicated employees hesitate ever to take a break because, as they see it, "Animals are dying while I sit here"—so says Laura Maloney, chief operating officer at the Humane Society of the United States. She adds, "We struggle to say, 'It's OK to take time off and replenish and rebuild.' Instead, the attitude is, 'We have to work every minute of every day,' and there can be a high burnout rate."

Some business leaders have become so worried about talent burnout that they are instituting policies that all but mandate time off.

At FullContact, a provider of cloud-based contact-management solutions, employees are actually paid to take vacation. Here's how the company website describes it:

*Not only do we provide employees minimum 15 days paid vacation plus the standard federal holidays, but **WE ALSO PAY FOR VACATIONS!** Here's how it works: Once per year, we give each employee **$7,500 to go on vacation.** There are a few rules:*

1. You have to go on vacation, or you don't get the money.

2. You must disconnect.

3. You can't work while on vacation.

The intent of the policy, obviously, is to get their people to take some time away from work in order to recharge and come back stronger than before. There is another motivation too: FullContact believes that if people know they will be going off the grid for an extended period each year, they will be less likely to fall victim to "hero syndrome," the mentality that says, "I'm the only one who can do this." This means, according to the company,

- They might empower direct reports to make more decisions.
- They might be less likely to create a special script that ... only lives on their machine.
- They might document their code a bit better.
- They might contribute to the company Wiki and share knowledge.

"At the end of the day," FullContact CEO and cofounder Bart Lorang concludes, "the company will *improve*."[9]

Other companies are likewise instituting policies intended to get notoriously vacation-hesitant American workers off the job. Employees at Airbnb get a $2,000 annual stipend to travel anywhere in the world they want.[10] At LoadSpring Solutions, a maker of project management software, employees who have been with the company for two years or longer receive $5,000, plus an extra week of vacation to travel overseas. "It sends a message to all new hires and employees in the company that we care about you and want you to get out and see the United States from another vantage point," founder and CEO Eric Leighton told *Inc Magazine*.[11]

We are also seeing the sabbatical move beyond the ivory tower to corporate America. In just two examples of this increasingly popular incentive, financial data firm Morningstar Inc. and 3-D design software company Autodesk both grant employees six weeks of paid leave after every four years of service. The Morningstar website explains, "We view the sabbatical program as a way of saying thanks for helping us grow, and as a way to help you grow."[12]

QUESTIONS TO ASK YOURSELF

- What else could you be doing to ensure your organization stands out as one flexible enough to meet the varied needs of the talent you seek?
- How could you more effectively prevent burnout and ensure your company benefits from fully motivated and engaged employees?
- Are you doing all you can to communicate to your talent that you care about them as people and are eager to help them find the right balance between work and the rest of their lives?

CHAPTER 15

TREAT YOUR TALENT RIGHT

THIS CHAPTER EXPLORES SOME MORE SPECIFIC THINGS you should be doing to support and encourage your best talent, right now. It is all about building a performance culture, one in which you are constantly on the lookout for top performers, rewarding them appropriately and often, and creating structures that give them everything they need to keep on performing well.

I have found that the following basic approaches and principles are the most critical attributes of such cultures:

1. Be a good boss, not a bad one.
2. Measure their progress.
3. Let them know they are making a difference.
4. Reward them creatively.
5. Boost their career trajectories.

These may seem obvious, but as the following sections will reveal, the devil is in the details.

BE A GOOD BOSS, NOT A BAD ONE

"Well, of course!" you are thinking; we all aspire to be good bosses. And yet how often people fail at this critical task. Put another way, think back on all the bosses you have had in your career. It's awfully easy to do this job wrong, isn't it?

That is a real problem, says John Costello at Dunkin' Brands Group, for numerous studies show that an individual's direct supervisor has a greater influence on his or her retention than any other factor. Costello believes more care needs to be put into training bosses to do their jobs right: "We need continuing education reoccurring at all levels concerning retention and the importance of talent. It is easy to assume top performers are also good leaders and developers of talent. Not so. We must train all supervisors so they understand that and use 360-degree ratings to make sure they are building strong relationships."

Heineken's Alexis Nasard warns that lousy managers can undermine motivation and rob talent of the peace of mind that allows them to focus on what is important. "If you are anxious, you will never take chances. If you feel you are working for a boss who is indifferent or does not care, you will feel insecure. And then you focus on not making mistakes instead of expanding the limits of what is possible."

In the past, we generally tolerated bad bosses as inevitable crags in the rocky business landscape, but those days are fast slipping away. Tomorrow's talent are cognizant of their value and are even more apt to jump ship over lack of recognition and appreciation than over issues related to compensation. That's right—the U.S. Department of Labor says that the number one reason people leave their jobs is because they "don't feel appreciated."

And as the economy rebounds, you should be worried about people leaving you. A 2012 survey showed that an extraordinary 51 percent of workers will consider looking for a new job if the economy stays the same or improves; another revealed that 19 million Americans definitely planned to leave their jobs in 2013.[1] It is wise to keep in mind the old axiom, "People don't leave jobs, they leave managers."

As for the workers who choose to remain with a bad boss, all too often their effectiveness is reduced to a devastating extent. Disengaged employees cost the U.S. economy $350 billion annually in lost productivity. A Wharton professor has argued that these laborers gradually lose vital abilities, including the capacity for "more flexible decision-making and wider search behavior and greater analytic precision."[2]

Bad bosses are choking off the lifeblood of American businesses. We need to get rid of them. Or, if you think you may be one of them, you need to turn your act around.

EMBRACE HIGH TOUCH

A top trait of good bosses these days is accessibility. You need to see and be seen, giving everyone explicit and implicit permission to engage with you about matters critical to the business. I have tried to stress high touch in my own companies, always being on the lookout for ways to exchange pronouncements-from-on-high for interchanges that are more conversational and personal. That's why, when we rolled out our newly articulated values at Arnold Worldwide, we did it through roundtables rather than a one-size-fits-all web conference. In this way, we got immediate feedback and were able to respond to whatever concerns were on people's minds.

Being a high-touch leader also means giving lots of feedback, even when it is not all positive. Remember, valuing people and having a caring environment is in no way incompatible with having a meritocracy and a performance-driven culture. Ultimately, people appreciate hearing how they are doing straight up. And they like to know that they will be rewarded for good performance. The problem too often is that people in management positions have not been properly trained to give effective feedback. The Weather Company's David Kenny sees this as a serious problem: "You make a lot more progress if you get data on how managers are developing their people. You have got to teach leaders how to develop their people. Many people are not good at this; they have been promoted because they are good at their job, but they don't know how to lead others."

CVS/pharmacy's Rob Price does not wait for formal reviews to let people know where they are falling short. He makes sure people understand that the feedback he provides is meant to be constructive not pointlessly critical:

> *I set a cultural expectation: "You are going to hear a lot of feedback from me. I am not doing it to make you feel bad." The feedback is organized by the topics in the annual goals. I do it because I know from experience that explicit, unvarnished feedback can be the absolute difference-maker for somebody's success, and it is in far too short supply. I have had great mentors who saved me from myself, who were generous enough to bang me over the head with a two-by-four and say, "This is a landmine for you." It has inspired me to be much more aggressive in soliciting feedback for myself, too.*

In building team culture, Price looks for "those individuals who are most capable of hearing feedback in the right spirit, without brittleness. Usually after several months of objective positive and negative feedback with a lot of clear context ('This is for you and your development'), employees come to value the approach." He makes sure to tell them, "'It is not a personal failing; it is a gap to fill.' I frequently tell stories about my own shortcomings, as analogies, with details that can even be somewhat uncomfortable to share." This approach shows employees that everyone is constantly developing at the company; everyone has room to improve.

Because ongoing assessments do not come naturally to all managers, we made it a point at Arnold to train leaders in how to give feedback and coach their team members more effectively. Thus far, a group of around 25 leaders have been put through our People Leadership Boot Camp, a two-day program designed to help them understand their management styles and learn how best to leverage these styles to get the most from their teams. Eventually, compensation will be tied to effective management practices. We intend to do the same at Havas Worldwide.

GIVE THEM A VOICE

Just as important as feedback from boss to worker is feedback running the other way. Good bosses in today's high-performance workplace actively solicit input from their direct reports and others. They open up a lively dialogue. "Every one-on-one I have with my team members, I am soliciting feedback," Rob Price told me.

In creating genuine, two-way feedback, it is also a good idea to use regular surveys to find out what your people are thinking and what needs improvement. Too often, businesses make a big production of a company-wide survey every few years, with no clear results stemming from it. It is far better to send briefer but more frequent surveys to get a sense of how things lie. And by brief, I mean *really* brief. Global management-consulting firm Bain & Company's Net Promoter System is centered on just one question: "What is the likelihood that you would recommend Company X to a friend or colleague?"[3]

MEASURE THEIR PROGRESS

Informal feedback is one thing; structured reviews are quite another. A great many businesses have a long way to go in this area, including my own. Regardless of whether we are comfortable conducting them, intelligent measurements of talent are critical, with the first step being to identify who your high performers actually are. Curiously, businesses often fail to notice which workers are doing extremely well at their jobs, says Colin Coulson-Thomas of the University of Greenwich: "My research shows that organizations are hugely bad at that—at identifying people who really make a contribution. . . . I see that in organization after organization. They aren't finding and supporting the people who really make the difference." He recommends involving peers in performance appraisals. The employee that a "manager might identify—because they look smart or they're always agreeing—may not really be the top performer. The peers themselves might say, actually that person didn't really contribute much at all, and we always used to go to and listen to someone else. They are the real star performers."

He believes strongly that companies need to find a way to identify those individuals who are falling through the cracks in addition to those who are important and significant: "And then you can provide them with support or more recognition. You're providing psychological motivational support."[4]

THE PROBLEM WITH PERFORMANCE REVIEWS

The subject of measuring talent leads us into the fetid swamps of "performance reviews," a term so laden with negative connotations that our chief talent officer, Patti Clifford, is rebranding it internally. When I brought Clifford to Havas Worldwide from Arnold, we were dismayed to find that many of our leaders bypass reviews entirely. "Giving feedback does not happen as much as it needs to," she says, "although team members are dying for it!" Why do these reviews matter so much? Without them, Clifford explains, we lose people—top talent who do not know how we feel about them. "They want to know: 'Am I doing well? What can I do better?' They want a dialogue with their leader." Clifford adds, "On the opposite end of the spectrum, you want to be documenting lower performers so that if they don't improve you can make the move to replace them."

By whatever name, she finds these reviews are not enormously popular with the people who are expected to give them. When she worked at Arnold, she recalls, "It took a lot of effort to get us to 80 percent of people having their reviews completed." Some bosses fail to offer feedback because they do not understand how to do it well. "Or they get wrapped up in the next thing, and it becomes easy to put aside as their plates are full." Plus they fear the awkward encounter: "The positive feedback is easier to give than the constructive." It is also common for managers to put off performance reviews because they have been linked in workers' minds with promotions and salary bumps. Businesses avoid them lest they have to start giving everybody raises.

Regardless of the effort required, Clifford advocates formal discussions between leaders and employees twice a year. This is done with the intent of pushing both the individual and the company to a better place. When there is resistance, she responds, "When done well, the preparation of the review and conversation shouldn't take more than three hours. Don't our team members deserve six hours' total annual investment in them?"

USING A CALIBRATION SESSION TO MEASURE TALENT

Let me explain more about the four-tier measuring system we instituted at Arnold Worldwide, borrowing an idea from McKinsey: the twice-annual talent assessment and calibration session. Every employee fell into a category. Although the percentages varied as our mix of talent changed, we typically identified around 20 percent as high performance, high potential; they were rewarded accordingly. Then there were the approximately 50 percent we called "steady contributors." We gave each of them guidance in their career paths, as well as training and development intended to help transform them into the type of rock stars we had in the top tier. For the 20 percent who needed extra work—the "counsel to improve" category—we mentored them, too, to boost their performance. The fundamental idea for all of the 90 percent of talent who fell into the top three tiers was to discover and then deliver what they needed to work at their optimal capacity. That left the 10 percent who fell into the "counsel to leave" group, those whose abilities and interests turned out to be an imperfect fit for our company. The reality is that, with resources so tight, clearing out the cupboards of underperforming talent is necessary to make room for others who will add more value.

All this is different, I believe, from what is being done elsewhere in the advertising industry, where talent management is, far too often, merely mechanized—not fully embraced as strategic and not being run as if it were a core competency of the company. And yet, as we have seen, that is precisely what it needs to be.

However you choose to do it, it is critical to measure progress. The alternative is disastrous: People are allowed to drift, and top performers go unrecognized. Every company needs to come up with measurements that work for them or risk losing workers who, sensibly enough, equate lack of feedback with lack of support, respect, and being valued.

LET THEM KNOW THEY ARE MAKING A DIFFERENCE

Motivating talent requires a lot more than signing a paycheck, although a big one of those certainly helps. In thinking about how to improve our talent management, I have asked these questions:

- Are our people truly being fulfilled?
- Are they using their aptitudes to the fullest?
- Are they being made to feel they count, that they are making a difference for the company?

Employees crave a sense of connectedness and purpose, intangible motivators considerably deeper and more subtle than financial remuneration. During his years with ExxonMobil, Stewart McHie found that "simply praising and recognizing was important. We got much better at recognizing people who were going the extra mile. It is like Maslow's theory of self-actualization: Everybody wants to feel they are adding value and contributing."

"In my experience, there are three important considerations to get the best people to stick with you," says Alexis Nasard at Heineken. First, "'Do I get to do what I'm best at?' Because if you do, it gives you a sense of progress every day, and you can see the results." At Heineken, Nasard points out, "There are no dogmatic views of what a role ought to be. People can bend their roles to what they are good at. This flexibility is priceless; it is a competitive advantage." Second: "'Is what I'm doing important for the company?' For talent to be attracted, it is important for them to feel that they are part of the bigger picture, and that what they do matters." He points out that P&G is particularly good at this: "They have everyone's work plans framed within the overall strategy for the company, no matter how junior the person is." And third: "'Does my boss care about me?' Working for a person who doesn't care can undermine any motivation you might have."

HAVE RECOGNITION COME EARLY AND OFTEN

It is never too early to let your talent know you are glad they are part of your team. Too many companies act as if they are doing a favor when hiring people, but if the hiring has been done right, the individuals have been chosen because they are going to make a real difference within the organization. Let them know that.

Some people-centered companies set the tone on day one, if not before. For instance, at the J. M. Smucker Company, new hires are welcomed with a gift basket sent to their homes.[5] At Intel, in addition to the greeters and gifts that await incoming employees on their first day, recent hires actually get "to walk the red carpet—complete with photographers, journalists, and fans—and feel like a celebrity at the quarterly Red Carpet Experience."[6] Neither of these examples puts a significant drain on resources, but they are gestures that set the right tone and are certain to be remembered.

REWARD THEM CREATIVELY

Financial compensation will always be a hot-button issue in talent management, but it is far from the only type of compensation that you should be concerned with. Take some time to consider in what other ways you are letting people know they are valued.

Life coach and All Access Group chief executive Kelli Richards sees a trend among her clients. "There is more receptivity to softer, intangible motivators," more recognition of the fact that "acknowledging people in front of their peers, offering flextime, giving more vacation time, these things make a huge difference. Savvy employers are aligning with the flexibility people want. From an attraction and retention standpoint, they are waking up to that. Because it directly correlates to productivity." Richards also cautions that any standardized policy cannot hope to meet the needs of our disparate workforces: "People want a sense of personal fulfillment and acknowledgment. Autonomy, passion, purpose—those are the motivators for people as individuals. You cannot take a cookie-cutter approach; people are not cookies. You cannot treat them all the same way."

That individualized approach can be seen at Kaufer Miller Communications, a small communications agency in Washington State. Cofounder David Kaufer tells of an employee who was suffering from a long commute. To help him out, Kaufer allowed him to work four ten-hour workdays, with Fridays off, until he could find a closer residence. "He really appreciates the three hours a day he doesn't have to spend on I-5," says Kaufer—a modest gesture, perhaps, but decidedly meaningful to that individual employee who, without it, might have sought a job elsewhere.[7]

Detailing all the creative ways in which organizations are recognizing talent would require a book of its own, so I will just share a couple of specific thoughts here: make it personal and consider getting peers involved. Two of the business leaders with whom I spoke mentioned the value of the handwritten note, a value that has increased sharply in our age of digital everything:

- "If you authentically show you care about employees, they will care for the company, for the mission, and be passionate about it," says Care.com's Sheila Marcelo. The day we spoke, she told me, "I got up at four o'clock this morning and wrote personal notes to employees."
- Many Citi staff faithfully went to work during Superstorm Sandy, although their own homes were at risk, Bob O'Leary told me. "So my team and I got the list of names and wrote personal notes to everyone who went beyond the call of duty. It was two hours around a conference table. It can be that simple. People want to be thanked and acknowledged. I tell you, those notes made a big difference."

Recognition from the boss is apt to be much appreciated but so are kudos from peers. At Dow, everyone has access to an online Recognition@Dow tool, with which they can celebrate colleagues' day-to-day contributions and milestone results. The highest level of this program is the Diamond Keepsake Award, which rewards employees for extraordinary initiatives with a cash bonus equal to 30 percent of their monthly pay.[8]

Another program at Dow that I particularly like is the Transformation in Action award. All too often, companies celebrate their technological superstars while overlooking the vital role of managerial and people skills and the everyday heroes who drive the culture of an organization. Not so at Dow. Any employee at the company may be nominated for one of these prestigious awards, which each year honor those who embody the company's four core competencies: leadership, creating customer value, driving innovation, and collaboration.

Being highly public with your recognition will definitely boost its value. Randy Altschuler told me that at CloudBlue they have a monthly company-wide phone call that recognizes people in different categories for their performance and rewards them with electronic gifts and shout-outs in front of the entire company. Intuit recognizes talent with the Spotlight Award (cash awards sent via email), gift cards, dinners with the executive team, and adding their names to the Innovation Wall of Fame.[9]

Some might suggest that the current uptick in recognition and rewards is being driven by millennials impatient for more "trophies," like those that line the shelves of their childhood bedrooms back home. But I tend to agree with succession-planning expert William J. Rothwell, who notes that all employees have shifted toward such demands as a result of companies' aggressive downsizing in recent years: "They want immediate rewards for good performance because they distrust their employers' abilities to award them in the future for hard work performed in the present."[10]

Don't make the mistake of waiting for your talent to announce their intention to leave before you express your appreciation. By that time, it will be too late.

WHEN PERKS ARE MORE THAN JUST PERKS

Many business leaders would label perks as expendable, the first things to go when purse strings are drawn tight. And in some situations, I would agree. Hosting a lavish holiday party while layoffs are looming is seldom a good idea. But perks can be a relatively cost-effective way to set an upbeat tone for a business and express not just appreciation for the talent that underpins the company but also a recognition of the authentic human beings behind the employee IDs. In industries with the most difficult to capture talent, the extras really do matter—especially for millennials, who value them greatly.

Nowhere is the fight to retain millennial talent more ferocious than in Silicon Valley. To understand what is happening there, I spoke with Tomer Kagan at Quixey. "In the Valley," Kagan says, "there is a huge demand for engineers, and there is almost a war of who has the better culture and perks and better work environment." College kids—top engineering students—spend their senior year flying around the country to interview at companies that pick them up in a limo and give them $300 dinners and a free Xbox just for interviewing. As a result, Kagan says, "These guys think of themselves as a valuable asset. They know they can snap their fingers and get ten offers. In hiring, our conversations are not so much about money or equity as, 'What is the work environment? What is the food like—who is your caterer, who is your chef?' It is at that level." While some may consider such millennials overindulged, these employers recognize the tremendous value of attracting scarce talent and know that the extras they provide will give them a vital edge.

The nascent Quixey firm—where the average employee age is about 28—does its best to stand out. Kagan works hard to ensure that Quixey offers a lively learning environment and that there is plenty of room for growth. "The people we interview ask, 'What is the type of work I'm going to be doing?' They want to be doing something mentally challenging. And they want to be part of our vision." Beyond that, though, "it is important that we promote a unique cultural experience," says Kagan.

"There is yoga going on right now in the main hall. We promote a people-come-first perspective and try to lower the friction between life and work. We are near a public transit hub. We serve breakfast, lunch, and dinner every day." And that's not all: "If you are an engineer, you can get any equipment you need," says Kagan. "We have personal trainers who come to the office. We have many speakers; we hire advisors and top technical experts for employees to work with. We have seven employee groups, from an improv team to a meditation group."

Kagan's efforts to enliven the culture seem to have paid off. Quixey has grown explosively, from three employees in 2011 to sixty in spring 2013.

BOOST THEIR CAREER TRAJECTORIES

Now that every employee is so vital—thanks, as we have seen, to downsizing, fiendish competition, and the need to squeeze every ounce of value out of everything—it only makes sense that companies are getting more serious about giving talent the support and tools they need to advance their careers. McKinsey invests in developing people even before a current student or experienced professional is hired, says Michael Zea. During the recruiting process, he explains, "It is immediately apparent that helping you is a top priority." Candidates are given resources to help them prepare for and practice their interview and case study skills, including sample cases, interview tips, and, where possible, live case coaching sessions. After the interview, each candidate also receives feedback on his or her performance. "People feel they are important and given their best chance to succeed."

It may not be practical for you to boost your talent's careers before they have even been given an offer, but there is plenty you can, and should, be doing once they have been assigned a desk.

DON'T SKIMP ON TRAINING AND OPPORTUNITIES FOR GROWTH

In the world of business past, says Walt Freese, "the contract was, the company provided value in the form of a paycheck and a bonus and potential for promotion. Today, employees expect that they will be trained, developed, and truly will be able to say, 'I'm going to come out of this job better.'"

Freese is exactly right. Once good prospects are on board, you will need to invest in their careers by exposing them to new developmental experiences and having them participate in training initiatives. And yet few companies do that well. Moreover, "Since it is not always done in a way that allows the organization to see a return on investment, it is easy to cut when times are tight," says Havas Worldwide's Patti Clifford. "Training needs to be accompanied by quantitative follow-up measurements, or it will sit on the chopping block. At Dun & Bradstreet [where she worked as senior vice president and chief human resources officer], we would track how many of our sales trainees later met their objectives."

Organizations that show admirable devotion to the training of their talent include Mercedes-Benz USA, which offers 175 instructor-led training sessions annually, more than 250 e-courses, and up to $8,000 per year in tuition reimbursement.[11] It may surprise you that another great example is found in supermarket retail: Wegmans, which operates 79 stores across the East Coast. The family-owned grocery chain manages to train its workforce in a way that leads to loyalty on the part of both employees and customers and to handsome profits. Its butchers are sent to Colorado, Uruguay, and Argentina to learn about beef, while its deli managers immerse themselves in cheese culture in places like Wisconsin, Italy, and France. And cashiers? They are not even allowed to interact with customers until they have had 40 hours of training. Is it any wonder Wegmans has half the turnover of its competitors? It is also a regular on *Fortune*'s lists of the best places to work.[12]

GIVE THEM A COACH

Coaches, advisors, sponsors, mentors—by whatever name they are known, it is an excellent idea to partner your talent with more experienced people who can guide their career paths. Some examples of smart companies doing it right:

- At Care.com, Sheila Marcelo takes two meals a month with star employees or with anyone who needs coaching in the area of career development. They have also invested in an executive coach who helps the management team and organizes team-building events.

- Google has career gurus who offer one-on-one career coaching sessions. One report explains, "Employees across the company can enroll in these highly focused and confidential career conversations with senior Google leaders. Engineering employees at all levels get advice and guidance from 'EngAdvisors,' senior leaders who are conversant in such topics as work-life balance, personal and professional development, role and location transfers, communication styles, performance reviews and conflict resolution."[13]

- Every employee at Gore-Tex maker W. L. Gore & Associates has a sponsor, "the go-to resource for any and all questions, feedback, or guidance on development opportunities. Sponsors also act as an advocate during the compensation process, ensuring that their associate's contributions are recognized. Ultimately, a sponsor ensures an associate's successful, long-term integration into his or her own role and into the Gore culture as a whole."[14]

PROMOTE THEM

Once you have identified and mentored your talent—and trained them generously—you should promote them, the University of Greenwich's Colin Coulson-Thomas says. In *Talent Management 2* (Policy Publications, 2012), he argues against a strong focus on recruitment, saying his research has found that much money is wasted on bringing in overpriced talent rather than better preparing existing talent for bigger roles:

> *We need to shift the emphasis from recruiting and developing high fliers for an unknown future to helping people to excel at activities that are crucial today and to handle challenges as, when and wherever they arise. . . . Talent*

wars to attract "the best people" can push up salary costs, be distracting and involve collateral damage. . . . It may be cheaper to work with the people one has and put the right support environment in place to enable them to succeed.[15]

His advice: Turn the people you have into high performers. Give them the support they need to do complex and difficult jobs. "To take a simple but powerful example," he says, "if you look at the World Health Organization checklist for operations, they just gave surgeons a piece of paper listing what the most successful surgeons do differently in operations. And when they did that it reduced in-patient deaths by a very significant amount."[16] Companies can turn average performers into something far more valuable by taking the time and care to support their performance.

QUESTIONS TO ASK YOURSELF

- How certain are you that you could identify accurately those employees who are most vital to your organization's success? What more should you be doing to acknowledge and reward them?
- What percentage of your managers do you believe are truly excellent bosses? What needs to happen to bring the others up to speed?
- How are you letting your talent know their contributions are vital to the organization? How are you motivating them to continue to give their all?
- What more could you do to foster career growth and turn your organization into a more self-sufficient place that does not rely on bringing in overpaid superstars?

STRATEGY SIX

MAKE IT MEAN SOMETHING

CHAPTER 16

DEFINE YOUR
HIGHER PURPOSE

We get to do things I would never have imagined had I not been hired here. Things that matter. Things that inspire people. Things that change our perception of our life on Earth and our place in the universe.[1]

THOSE ARE THE WORDS OF STEVEN COWART, DESCRIBING his job. Can your employees voice this kind of boundless enthusiasm? Well, probably not. Cowart is manager for visual display systems at NASA. Some organizations are, by their nature, rich with deeper meaning. But I urge you to think about exactly what Cowart said: *He gets to do things that matter* because a certain employer hired him—things that inspire, things that make a difference. And these are higher-minded approaches that many companies can successfully emphasize today—even without sending their employees beyond the surly bonds of Earth.

Twenty-first-century workers crave connection—to a bigger picture, to a cause, to a crusade even. The very best talent are no longer satisfied with just collecting a paycheck or earning the corner office. They are asking themselves, "Do I have reason to be proud of my company? Am I doing something worthwhile?"

That is the way Steve Jobs famously lured John Sculley to work for him at Apple—asking the Pepsi-Cola CEO, "Do you want to spend the rest of your life selling sugared water, or do you want a chance to change the world?"

So how do you reshape your talent approach so that you are paying sufficient attention to the current employee's hunger for meaning? It is a three-part process:

1. Establish your higher purpose.
2. Engage your talent in the higher purpose.
3. Inspire your talent by driving change in the world.

ESTABLISH YOUR HIGHER PURPOSE

It is no coincidence that three of the most talked-about companies of this new century were all built with a proud, overarching purpose that extends beyond their product lines and services. Google's mission is "to organize the world's information and make it universally accessible and useful." Facebook, in the words of founder Mark Zuckerberg, aims "to make the world more open and connected."[2] And while Apple's current mission statement is bland (focusing on product lines), the 1980 version conceived by Steve Jobs was lofty in the extreme: "To make a contribution to the world by making tools for the mind that advance humankind."[3]

New hires at Apple are told that they are embarking on a thrilling mission: "*Amaze yourself. Amaze the world.* A job at Apple is unlike any other you've had. You'll be challenged. You'll be inspired. And you'll be proud. Because whatever your job is here, you'll be part of something big."[4] Notice how this language deliberately is crafted to emphasize the heady idea of "higher purpose."

I spoke with San Francisco State University's John Sullivan about the impact of this sense of purpose on Apple. He told me that CEOs ask him all the time, "Why can't I be like Apple?" He counsels them, "Apple has a harsh environment. It never makes the 'best places to work' list. There is no free food, there is incredible secrecy, teams cannot talk to each other. But people want to work there to make 'wow' products, to do the best work of their lives. So it is not about hugging people or being nice to them." Instead, it is about giving them a chance to do important things.

John Sculley told me that employees everywhere want "what Steve Jobs used to call the Noble Cause. Often that is an even bigger attractor than the money." What Sculley looks for at the company helm: "Does a leader have the ability to articulate a noble cause that will be inspiring?" He says that too often people mistake high intelligence for leadership potential. "Just being smart is no big deal. That's not a big advantage. Being smart and having a great idea, that's not unique either. I look for a leader who has the ability to be inspiring regarding what they are trying to do."

Obviously, not all companies can offer a reinvent-the-world mission on the level of Apple or Google, but all can take steps to articulate clearly how their work is a noble enterprise that is worth being part of. The business world abounds with utterly meaningless—and laughably bad—statements of vision, but plenty of companies have also succeeded in crafting statements that are clear, concise, and fully capable of rallying the troops. A few of my favorites:

- "To instantly connect people everywhere to what's most important to them" (Twitter)
- "To inspire and nurture the human spirit—one person, one cup and one neighborhood at a time" (Starbucks)
- "Helping people around the world eat and live better" (Kraft Foods)
- "Every book ever printed, in any language, all available in less than 60 seconds" (Amazon's Kindle)

Notice how these statements come from a variety of businesses doing different types of work, and yet all refer to big, even universal themes that are tied in to their unique product offerings. Instinctively, each company followed the advice of nineteenth-century Chicago architect Daniel Burnham: "Make no little plans; they have no magic to stir men's blood."

ENGAGE YOUR TALENT IN THE HIGHER PURPOSE

Defining your higher purpose is a start. But to have a noble cause that genuinely inspires and energizes your talent, you have to let them contribute to that purpose and, just as important, make them really feel that they are contributing. The payoff may surprise you.

Recently, Temkin Group surveyed almost 2,500 full-time workers in the United States and compared the attitudes of two cohorts: those who find their company's mission inspiring and those who do not. They found that members of the former group are far more likely to:

- Do something that's good for the employer, even if it wasn't requested of them
- Help a co-worker out without being asked to do so
- Work late
- Recommend the employer to a friend looking for a job
- Make a suggestion about an improvement that might help the company[5]

The researchers' conclusion: "Inspired employees are a huge asset." If your mission is not inspirational, you are not benefiting from a fully engaged and committed workforce.

Sometimes the link between what an employee does each day and what the company as a whole accomplishes is a bit fuzzy, and so smart companies are finding ways to expose these vital connections to workers. I like the example of ServiceMaster, which manages janitorial, laundry, and other support services for hospitals, schools, and other institutions. According to one report, ServiceMaster "emphasizes the contribution each server makes to the end customer. For example, a physician might be asked to address hospital janitorial staff on how a sanitary and neat room improves patients' recovery chances." An executive has said, "We have housekeepers relating to their task and saying, 'Hey, I've got something to do with that person being well.' . . . [Our people] work better when they understand the value of their contribution."[6]

MINIMIZE THE DISCONNECT

Not every task will offer a direct link to the organization's higher purpose, but companies I admire are taking steps to consciously redistribute or minimize assignments that do not engage their talent in that purpose.

At Quixey, Tomer Kagan explained to me why ambitious people so often want to work at a startup instead of a big company: "They're looking for a culture where they can be close to the product itself, where they will have an impact. They want a very good learning environment for themselves. There is more room for growth here, and you'll be closer to the vision. The people we interview ask, 'What is the type of work I'm going to be doing? Will it be mentally challenging?'"

But surely all work is not challenging and interesting? "We make sure they share the load on the boring stuff, switch it around, so nobody gets really stuck with it."

I heard much the same from Dan Clifford of AnswerLab. "It is core to the culture of the company that people want to learn new things, take on new challenges." They have even turned down lucrative contracts that would have subjected employees to mind-numbing, repetitious work for a month, Clifford says. "That's one lesson I've learned: being true to core values even in saying 'no' to certain things. It shows the team we really care about our values."

There will always be boring tasks, but fewer and fewer workers are willing to spend the preponderance of their careers shoveling muck or, like Sculley, selling sugared water when they could be changing the world. As never before, they crave connection to a big picture and a higher cause.

INSPIRE YOUR TALENT BY DRIVING
CHANGE IN THE WORLD

Increasingly often these days, a company's higher purpose is tied to solving some critical issue the world faces. Many CEOs have discovered that engaging their workforces in socially responsible activities boosts employees' skills, job satisfaction, and loyalty to the company—as well as the bottom line. It powerfully involves those institutions in a web of potent connections, says Walt Freese: "Companies are increasingly making the connection between culture, values, talent, and society. And the ones who don't are going to pay the price: They will be losing talent."

Attitudes in this regard have changed radically in a short time. Not long ago, corporate social responsibility (CSR) was widely regarded as a sop to bleeding hearts who did not understand the real world, the difficult exigencies of running a profitable business. But today companies everywhere are scrambling to burnish their images as solid corporate citizens. Fully 95 percent of Fortune 250 companies now release an annual social responsibility report, and many other companies include CSR credentials as part of their "about us" information.

In fighting the talent wars, is heavy investment in a purpose beyond profits really worth it? Here I offer three reasons that you ought to answer "yes":

1. Driving change will burnish your reputation.
2. Driving change galvanizes millennials.
3. Driving change can improve your talent's skills.

DRIVING CHANGE WILL BURNISH YOUR REPUTATION

In 2012, Havas Worldwide conducted a survey of more than 10,000 adults in 31 countries to better understand people's expectations regarding corporate conduct and responsibility. Around three-quarters of respondents (73 percent) believe that the more powerful corporations become, the more they are obligated to behave ethically and with the public interest in mind. More than two-thirds (69 percent) said businesses have a responsibility to drive change. Incredibly, just about as many, 68 percent, actually believe that businesses bear as much responsibility as government for driving social change. And 76 percent look to corporations and government to work together to improve conditions globally.

A growing number of companies are paying attention to such attitudes, cognizant of the increasingly clear correlation between reputation and profitability. According to our research, two-thirds of consumers are paying more attention now to the environmental and social impact of the products they buy, and around six in ten prefer to buy from companies that share their personal values.

Moreover, the pride that workers take in their employers' CSR actions directly affects their job performance and satisfaction. In a study by the Society for Human Resource Management, firms with strong sustainability programs were compared with ones without such programs. The prosustainability camp enjoyed 55 percent better employee morale, 43 percent more efficient business processes, 38 percent stronger employee loyalty, and a 43 percent better public image. Clearly, what you do with regard to responsibility bears fruit in many ways, including with your talent.[7]

"CSR is a smart thing for any business with an eye on regulatory and consumer issues, but it also makes good business sense," affirms Walt Freese. "Authenticity becomes absolutely key. If the commitment is really just a commitment to your bottom line, that is going to be very transparent to employees and consumers. At Ben & Jerry's, we weren't allowed to say 'brand positioning.' Instead, it was 'authenticity.' And that resonates with consumers, who are, after decades of exposure to advertising, extremely good at discerning what's authentic and what is positioning."

DRIVING CHANGE GALVANIZES MILLENNIALS

Unilever's Paul Polman is a vocal advocate of sustainable and equitable business models. It is his firm conviction that companies with a robust social mission are not just doing the "right thing" but that they will be more financially successful over the long term as a result. He notes the import of a higher purpose to all employees but in particular to millennials: "For younger people today, a higher purpose is of paramount importance. They care about the future and their company's role in it—and they are genuinely worried about the direction in which the world is going. And they *should* worry about it and be passionate about driving change and pushing companies to do good: They will be the ones living in it!"

At Unilever, Polman says, "We look to provide solutions that will drive social change. We believe that companies that empower the young and leverage social media will galvanize change and create positive social movements." In 2012, Unilever won the first FTSE4Good Sir Mervyn Pedelty Award, which recognizes companies that integrate environmental and social performance into business strategy.

Dave Lewis, president of the personal care division at Unilever, sees a clear impact of the company's socially responsible activities on talent: "Interestingly, an increasing proportion of people that I meet with today initiate the conversation around purpose and values. It is as important to them as it is to us. We used to have a problem with satisfying our people's needs for career mobility. They would want to do well on a brand, then move on to a bigger challenge. Today, increasingly, we have people so personally invested in the purpose of their brands that they don't want to move off. They care deeply about what they're doing and want to see it through."

Lewis cites as an example global brand vice president Samir Singh, who has spearheaded Lifebuoy's Help a Child Reach 5 hand-washing campaign, designed to keep young children from succumbing to preventable diseases such as diarrhea and pneumonia. Every year, such diseases kill some two million children under the age of five. As part of the Unilever campaign, Singh and his team created a three-minute film depicting a father's poignant celebration of his son's fifth birthday. The film quickly exceeded six million views on YouTube and has driven many of those viewers to a pledge drive on Facebook. "Our brief was to translate the statistic of this mortality rate into something real, personal, and powerful,"

Singh explains. "And through this film, that's just what has been done. Our goal is to raise awareness and change the hand-washing behaviors of a billion people by 2015."

Earlier, I mentioned Daniel Maree, a senior global digital strategist at Havas Worldwide. He is also a filmmaker, writer, and social activist known for organizing (with the support of his employer at the time) the Million Hoodies movement after the 2012 shooting death of hoodie-wearing Florida teenager Trayvon Martin. In common with many of his fellow millennials, Maree's passion for driving change is palpable:

I believe that, as advertisers, we are cultural engineers and have the capacity to create demand for causes. The added value of a global agency is to work with global clients. That is promising for creating real change. We place social good at the very center of the work that we do, and that is incredibly important to me. Many agencies talk about doing that, but there is no real commitment. When you put social good at the core of what you do, it really drives business growth. It can be a huge profit machine, even as it helps society.

Maree adds that creating shared value is not the old CSR: "It's not a PR stunt and looking good. Because that doesn't help anybody; it doesn't create business growth and it doesn't help society." The new, more authentic ways of creating real shared value are incredibly attractive to millennials, he observes. Following the Million Hoodies campaign, he has spoken widely. "All the students I have spoken to over the past year, the thing I have heard the most is: We want to know how we can work for a company that allows something like that to materialize."

If you are going to make your business attractive to the next generation of talent, you have to embrace a culture of change-making. Take note: A 2012 study by Net Impact and Rutgers University found that more than 70 percent of college students—and 50 percent of workers generally—are looking for jobs that have a social impact.[8]

Empowering Millennials Through One Young World

I believe that professionals within our industry are not only uniquely suited but also especially obligated to drive positive change. As our global CEO David Jones said, "What our industry excels at isn't just advertising or communications, but changing people's behavior. We have not only an opportunity, but an obligation to use this talent to change people's behavior around some of the bigger issues facing the world."

We do this by applying our best creative thinking to the compelling issues of the day. Our most ambitious initiative to date is One Young World, created by Jones and our UK group chairman Kate Robertson to "empower tomorrow's leaders to change the world today." Every year since 2010, more than one thousand young activists (aged 25 and younger) have been nominated by leaders in business, government, and the non-profit sector to attend a multiday summit in a different world capital. Delegates are selected on the basis of their record of community involvement, commitment to solving global issues, and leadership skills.

The young delegates attend presentations and workshops led by highly esteemed counselors from around the globe. In the first three years, these counselors have included Nobel Peace Prize winners Desmond Tutu, Kofi Annan, and Muhammad Yunus, musician-activist Bob Geldof, former U.S. president Bill Clinton, and business leaders Paul Polman (Unilever) and Antony Jenkins (Barclays). Once back home, the delegates work on ambassador projects they have devised to address the issues they feel most passionate about such as healthcare, education, or the environment. To date, One Young World has spawned hundreds of ambassador projects and has become an admired force for change.

One Young World always proves a life-enhancing experience for those selected to take part, and it has also had a palpable impact on our company, both because of the collective pride we take in its success (it has been dubbed the "Junior Davos" by CNN) and because of the hard work and passion so many of our employees put into the program each year. Many of our younger workers have attended as delegates. It is a great way for us—as a company and as individuals committed to socially responsible change—to get hands-on experience in the sorts of worthy work we so often recommend to clients. One of our employee delegates, associate director of global talent Allison Ciummei, had this to say upon her return from the 2013 forum in Pittsburgh:

> *I went into One Young World with a very open mind—hoping to get ideas about how people are making an impact on the world, through their work. The one thing that really resonated with me was the idea that "big isn't always bad." Working in a large company, we can sometimes feel like our size limits us from having a heart, when in reality our size and global presence should be two things that allow us to make a greater positive impact on the world. Following One Young World, I have taken even more of an interest in building stronger connections between global offices—not only to improve the work we do for our clients, but more importantly, the work we do as global citizens.*

DRIVING CHANGE CAN IMPROVE YOUR TALENT'S SKILLS

Active involvement in altruistic social causes will not just improve your reputation among consumers but actually can boost your employees' skills. Some companies are finding that sending employees overseas to pursue socially responsible activities has the added benefit of preparing them for today's truly global business environment. IBM is one of those companies. Since 2008, it has spent an estimated $5 million a year to send some 1,400 employees on CSR assignments overseas, helping, for example, to reform Kenya's postal system and develop ecotourism in Tanzania. Big Blue credits the program with helping to generate millions of dollars in new business overseas.[9]

Pharmaceutical giant Pfizer reports that some of the 270 employees it has sent abroad on CSR assignments describe the experience as a "mini-MBA." Caroline Roan, vice president of corporate responsibility, says participants "build skills, in part because they are sometimes thrust into situations outside of their comfort zone, which tends to make people more creative."[10]

Driving Change in Africa While Bonding with PepsiCo

I am a fan of PepsiCo's approach to talent and especially of the work chairman and chief executive officer Indra K. Nooyi has done in that regard. I cannot think of any other CEO of a global conglomerate who would take the time to write to her top executives' parents to thank them for the excellent job they did in raising their children.

In one of many innovative initiatives, the company has created PepsiCorps, a program through which "the future leaders of PepsiCo . . . use their business skills and expertise to gain insights into community and consumer needs while tackling real-world societal challenges." In 2011, a team flew to Ghana to improve access to clean water there. A year later, the company announced that the program would expand to 16 associates, with half working on a clean water project in India and the other half focusing on a sustainable agriculture or health and nutrition project on a Native American reservation in the United States.

There is a compelling approach here concerning talent. The company is singling out its best and brightest employees for these teams and, in so doing, forging deeper bonds between them and the organization. As Nooyi explained at a forum at Boston College,

> *I want the emotional bond to be strong. . . . One of the things we've discovered is young people, in particular, like to get involved in projects that . . . make a difference to the world. . . . The high potential people can apply for a seat on PepsiCorps, and we're going to send them off to Ghana . . . to do some projects that give them a great feeling about participating in something through PepsiCo to change the world.*[11]

This is effective CSR in action: driving change planet-wide while strengthening the talent picture back home.

It is not easy to develop socially minded programs that are both meaningful and effective, but these will pay great dividends in keeping your talent fresh and motivated. Today's workers crave connection to a higher purpose, and the best companies are going to extraordinary lengths to provide it.

QUESTIONS TO ASK YOURSELF

- How could you more clearly articulate your organization's mission and vision to your employees and outside stakeholders?
- What more can you do to ensure all employees feel they are making a genuine contribution to that mission through their work?
- How can you reduce or more equitably distribute the burden of tasks that threaten to disengage your talent from the company's mission?
- What more could you do to offer your talent the inspiring chance to drive change in the world?

PART III

CONCLUSION

CHAPTER 17

A TALENT UTOPIA

We used to outsource the recruitment of our people. Now it is a core aspect of what all of our leaders do. I spend a great amount of my time meeting people, bringing diverse perspectives into Unilever. Putting people first is central to our business.

—*Paul Polman, CEO, Unilever*

I WROTE THIS BOOK BECAUSE I WAS DEEPLY DISSATISFIED with the talent situation in my own industry and hoped to define the many ways in which it needs to be improved. I quickly learned that talent is a troubled aspect of modern corporate life in general. Too often it receives insufficient attention from the smart people at the top of the organization. Their thinking is short term, often quarter to quarter, and does not place sufficient emphasis on talent as the great driver of long-term success.

I have a vision of a future in which talent is put front and center, properly regarded as central to the business of making money, growing the company, and expanding its reach and influence within the larger community. Through talent, I believe, all things are possible.

What would this ideal future look like? On a long transatlantic flight to the international headquarters of Havas in Paris, looking out at the cold blue curve of the Atlantic beneath a nearly black sky, I mused on this question.

If I were to imagine that talent utopia of tomorrow, where all the right conditions had been established, all the wisest dictates followed, it might look something like the following. Here is the future I envision.

CONCERNING THE BUSINESS ITSELF

1. *The organization embraces a higher purpose.* The hard work we did with our values at Arnold Worldwide has paid off in helping every worker orient toward a polar star of definite truth in this world of flux and confusion. So I hope every company will have values and stick with them in an authentic way. The high mission will be communicated clearly and often to fundamentally explain why the employees come to work every day, thereby ensuring talent are constantly inspired.

2. *The business connects with the community.* And not just in token gestures—instead, the work of the company is reconceived in light of the larger societal good. Every organization can contribute in some useful way that will infuse talent with a sense of greater impact, of contributing to a cause greater than their personal paycheck.

3. *The office is a highly functional family.* In the future, corporate cultures will be nurtured carefully and shepherded so that workers feel supported and secure. In such an environment, they will be emboldened to make daring decisions and take entrepreneurial risks. They will have the freedom and motivation to grow toward their highest possible levels of accomplishment.

4. *The workforce is a team.* Or a score of teams—the whole approach to solving problems will be deliberately team based, teams both multigenerational and multifunctional. Mixing the digitally savvy with the more traditionally experienced talent can produce bold innovations that are rooted in sound practice, with good odds for success.

CONCERNING THE HIRING PROCESS

5. *Hiring looks to the future.* As talent is evaluated throughout the initial interview, they will be gauged by future potential more than by past experience. And, paradoxically, they will be regarded favorably for having made past mistakes: In a world marked by exponential change, risk-taking and recovery from failure are critical skills. Those who are hiring will take chances on talent who, even if they lack the perfectly square background for the square hole, display promising attributes that bode well for future success, including passion, flexibility, and a high degree of intuition.

6. *Hiring favors generalists.* Liberal arts majors who have studied past events—peering around the corner of yesterday—are uniquely suited to the wizardry of peering around the corner of tomorrow, a skill we all need right now. And even in the hiring of specialists and technicians, greater attention will be paid to their breadth of attributes, to their ability to interact effortlessly with teams and with diverse customers and to communicate concepts fluently in the burgeoning ideas economy.

7. *Hiring looks within.* Encouraging your workers to stay with you because of the opportunities available to them will be easier once clear pathways are established for progressing upward or laterally within the company. Increased training and attention to broadening every worker will prepare them well for heightened responsibility. Consistently hiring from within will help build a culture that is both unified and forward thinking.

CONCERNING BOSSES

8. *Managers will be people-developers.* No longer will workers be promoted into management without having received extensive training concerning talent management. No longer will managers conceive their role narrowly, as ensuring that certain tasks are neatly done and checkmarks filled in. Instead, they will see for themselves a far

broader role, as facilitators of the personal growth of each person under their charge.

9. *The boss will become the coach.* If the workforce is to be a team, managers will need to redefine themselves as coaches of that team, with a concomitant reevaluation of their entire style and approach. Their job will now be to bring out the best in every employee by a thorough evaluation of their strengths and weaknesses, with clear plans developed for future achievement, just as a track coach might do with a young athlete. This requires patience, dedication, intuition—all attributes that future bosses will deliberately inculcate in themselves.

10. *No jerks allowed.* With teamwork placed front and center and management reconceptualized as intelligent, compassionate coaching, the old-fashioned jerk will find himself with no role to play. That bullying style once so familiar in corporations will be shunned—rewarded not with promotion but with termination. The devastating impact of such people will be fully recognized: how they poison culture, stifle the growth of their reports, and drive good talent right out the door.

CONCERNING THE INDIVIDUAL WORKER

11. *Everybody's work will be made meaningful.* More responsibility will be pushed down to the middle tier: more crucial decision making and more of the kind of delegated management that the digital revolution has so powerfully fostered by putting vast data streams in the hands of all. Bosses will take care to rotate workers through varied roles and assignments so they do not grow bored or complacent, shifting them creatively across the lattice. This mixing up of the talent pool will usefully broaden the individual even as it lights the fires of synergistic thinking organization-wide, benefiting everybody.

12. *Engagement will be measured by results not the time clock.* A whole revolution will have unfolded here, as time itself is reconsidered.

Future workers (at least in jobs that do not inescapably require being in a set place at a set time) will work the hours of their choosing, connecting and disconnecting throughout fluid days and nights. There will be no pressure to punch a clock. Instead, everyone will be rewarded for delivering strong results. Freed from the old tyranny of time, they will develop their projects with a heightened sense of individual responsibility for outcomes.

13. *Everybody will be agile.* From day one on the job, workers will know that the new expectation is agility. They will each manage their personal brand, constantly keeping it fresh and up-to-date, through training that companies will provide. Everyone will assume that their current job may soon be obliterated by advances in technology or economic shifts—freeing them to jump into new tasks for which they have already laid the groundwork by careful preparation, in tandem with their mentor-managers.

CONCERNING THE C-SUITE

14. *The CEO will put talent first.* Nothing can happen—none of these exciting and promising events of the imaginary utopia I have outlined—without the wholehearted commitment of the top brass. They are the rudder that steers the ship.

HERE WE COME BACK TO THE FUNDAMENTAL MESSAGE OF this book. In an ideal future, the CEO will constantly think about talent issues. Driving his or her every decision will be the talent mandate, a conviction that long-term progress is impossible without first creating an environment in which every human being has an opportunity to expand and thrive. Tomorrow's CEO will recognize, at last, the fundamental premise that having the right people—and creating an environment in which they will flourish—is the prime differentiator between companies that will innovate and grow and those that are doomed to fail.

MEASURING SUCCESS THROUGH
THE TALENT IMPACT FUND

How does smart talent management translate into business performance? In an attempt to quantify it, my team and I pulled the top 25 publicly traded companies from *Fortune*'s 2013 list of 100 Best Companies to Work For.[1] We calculated the change in the prices of these stocks between May 2008[2] and May 2013 and then compared these with the change in the S&P 500 and Dow Jones indices over that period.

Over the five years, the S&P rose 20 percent, and the Dow Jones index increased 23 percent. And our talent impact fund? It grew 46 percent, more than double the rate of growth experienced by either of the other funds. This is what living a people-first culture can do for you.

Ahead of us, in the dark wood of a confusing environment beset by change, the road divides. I urge you to make the right choice—to follow the higher path that puts your people first, strengthening them for the challenges ahead and bringing out the best in their humanity. That is the path the wisest CEOs will choose, toward the constant and enthusiastic encouragement of their most valuable resource: their talent.

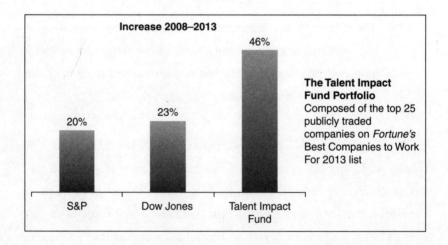

Increase 2008–2013

46%

23%

20%

S&P   Dow Jones   Talent Impact Fund

The Talent Impact Fund Portfolio
Composed of the top 25 publicly traded companies on *Fortune's* Best Companies to Work For 2013 list

NOTES

1 THE BIG SHIFT

1. Allison Linn, "Why Companies Aren't Hiring More Workers," MSNBC .com, August 4, 2011, http://www.nbcnews.com/id/44006656/ns/today -today_news/t/why-companies-arent-hiring-more-workers/.
2. Tom Peters, "The Brand Called You," *Fast Company*, August–September 1997, http://www.fastcompany.com/28905/brand-called-you.
3. Havas Worldwide Global Talent Study, April 2013.

2 SILICON VALLEY

1. "Triumph of the Nerds: Impressing Their Friends," 1996 PBS television documentary series, http://www.pbs.org/nerds/.
2. Havas Worldwide Global Talent Study, April 2013.
3. Steve Jobs, interview by Robert X. Cringely, 1995, http://www.magpictures .com/stevejobsthelostinterview/.

3 A NEW WAY TO WORK

1. Steve Jobs, Stanford University commencement address, June 12, 2005, http://news.stanford.edu/news/2005/june15/jobs-061505.html.
2. Allison Hillhouse, "Consumer Insights: MTV's 'No Collar Workers,'" October 4, 2012, http://blog.viacom.com/2012/10/consumer-insights-mtvs -no-collar-workers/.

3. Capstrat, "The Truth About Millennial Workers," 2011, http://www.capstrat .com/elements/downloads/files/millennials-work.pdf.

4. Gen Y Hub, "The New Workplace Currency," March 28, 2013, http:// genyhub.com/page/the-new-workplace-currency.

5. Future Workplace, "Multiple Generations @ Work" (survey of 1,189 knowl-edge workers, millennials, 91% of millennials expect to stay in a job for less than three years)," March 28, 2013, http://futureworkplace.com/speaking/.

6. Mr Youth and Intrepid Study, "What Your Company Will Look Like When Millennials Call the Shots," 2010, http://www.millennialinc.com/viewPaper .html.

7. Iconoculture, "Generations at Work," 2011, https://www.iconoculture.com /media/PDF/pd_GenerationsatWorkPDF_287508_2.pdf.

8. Pew, "Millennials Will Benefit and Suffer Due to Their Hyperconnected Lives," February 29, 2012, http://www.pewinternet.org/Reports/2012 /Hyperconnected-lives/Overview.aspx.

9. Cisco Connected Technology Report, "The Future of Work: Information Access Expectations, Demands, and Behavior of the World's Next-Generation Workplace," November 2, 2011, http://www.cisco.com/en/US/solutions /ns341/ns525/ns537/ns705/ns1120/cisco_connected_world_technology _report_chapter2_press_deck.pdf (p. 6; accessed March 28, 2013).

4 ATTEND TO YOUR DNA

1. *Fast Company*, "Culture Eats Strategy for Lunch," January 24, 2012, http:// www.fastcompany.com/1810674/culture-eats-strategy-lunch.

2. Havas Worldwide Global Talent Study, April 2013.

3. *Fortune*, "Southwest's Herb Kelleher: Still Crazy After All These Years," January 13, 2013, http://management.fortune.cnn.com/2013/01/14/kelleher -southwest-airlines/.

4. Havas Worldwide Global Talent Study, April 2013.

5 MEASURE TWICE, HIRE ONCE

1. Havas Worldwide Global Talent Study, April 2013.

2. 37signals, *Getting Real*, 2006, http://gettingreal.37signals.com/ch08_Kick _the_Tires.php.

3. "Top 25 Most Difficult Companies to Interview," July 27, 2012, http://www
.glassdoor.com/blog/top-25-difficult-companies-interview-consulting-firms
-lead/.

4. "How the Dream Works," CXO, http://www.cxo.eu.com/article/How-the
-dream-works/.

5. Zappos, "Zappos Family Core Values," April 2013, http://about.zappos.com
/our-unique-culture/zappos-core-values.

6. Bryan's Blog, "Delivering Loyalty: 10 Ways Zappos.com Creates Happy
Employees," November 12, 2012, http://pearson4loyalty.com/2012/11
/delivering-loyalty-10-ways-zappos-com-creates-happy-employees/.

6   EQUIP YOUR PLAYERS

1. DDI World, "How Employees View Leaders," 2011, http://www.ddiworld
.com/DDIWorld/media/go-magazine/gomagazine_v9n1_dm_ddi.pdf?ext=
.pdf (p. 11; accessed April 10, 2013).

2. Rackspace, "What's in the Rackspace Secret Sauce?" September 20, 2011,
http://www.rackspace.com/blog/whats-in-the-rackspace-secret-sauce/.

3. Valve Handbook for New Employees, 2012, http://assets.sbnation.com
/assets/1074301/Valve_Handbook_LowRes.pdf (p. 4).

4. Ibid. (p. 23).

5. Joe McKendrick, "A $4-Billion Company with No Managers? Can It Be?"
March 8, 2013, http://www.smartplanet.com/blog/bulletin/a-4-billion
-company-with-no-managers-can-it-be/14440?tag=content;siu-container.

7   TRUST THEM

1. The Great Place to Work Institute, "What Is a Great Workplace?" April 13, 2013,
http://www.greatplacetowork.com/our-approach/what-is-a-great-workplace.

2. Havas Worldwide Global Talent Study, April 2013.

3. Adam Lashinsky, "Larry Page: Google Should Be Like a Family," *Fortune*,
January 19, 2012, http://tech.fortune.cnn.com/2012/01/19/best-companies
-google-larry-page/.

4. Sam Cicotello, "A Culture of Trust," The Motley Fool, September 3, 2012,
http://culture.fool.com/2012/09/03/a-culture-of-trust/.

5. Ibid.

6. Alex Abraham, "By the Numbers: 50 Facts About Millennials," Edelman Digital, June 1, 2011, http://www.edelmandigital.com/2011/06/01/by-the -numbers-50-facts-about-millennials/.

7. Sam Cicotello, "A Culture of Trust," Motley Fool, September 3, 2012, http:// culture.fool.com/2012/09/03/a-culture-of-trust/.

8. Casey Hibbard, "How IBM Uses Social Media to Spur Employee Innovation," Social Media Examiner, February 2, 2010, http://www.socialmediaexaminer .com/how-ibm-uses-social-media-to-spur-employee-innovation/.

9. Adam Bryant, "Corner Office: Robert LoCascio—To Tear Down Walls, You Have to Move Out of Your Office," interview, *New York Times*, February 9, 2013, http://www.nytimes.com/2013/02/10/business/livepersons-chief-on -removing-organizational-walls.html?pagewanted=1&_r=0.

8   BE RELENTLESSLY ADAPTIVE

1. Nancy M. Davis, "DreamWorks Fosters Creativity, Collaboration, and Engagement," Society for Human Resource Management, July 5, 2012, http://www.shrm.org/publications/hrnews/pages/dreamworks.aspx.

2. Rieva Lesonsky, "Pearls of Wisdom," Entrepreneur.com, November 1, 2004, http://www.entrepreneur.com/article/73230#.

3. Globoforce, "Colin Coulson-Thomas Interview," http://www.globoforce .com/globoforce_colin_coulson_thomas_interview.

4. Diana Ransom, "The Rise of Entrepreneurship on College Campuses," *Young Entrepreneur*, December 20, 2012, http://www.youngentrepreneur .com/blog/startup-news/the-rise-of-entrepreneurship-on-college-campuses -infographic/.

9   CREATE AN INNOVATION-CENTERED WORKPLACE

1. "The World's Most Innovative Companies 2013," *Fast Company*, http://www .fastcompany.com/section/most-innovative-companies-2013.

2. Havas Worldwide Global Talent Study, April 2013.

3. Linus Carl Pauling, The Nobel Peace Laureate Project, www.nobelpeace laureates.org/pdf/Linus_Carl_Pauling.pdf.

4. Sam Cicotello, "A Culture of Trust," http://culture.fool.com/2012/09/03/a -culture-of-trust/.

5. Chuck Salter, "Failure Doesn't Suck," *Fast Company*, May 1, 2007, http:// www.fastcompany.com/59549/failure-doesnt-suck.

6. Dean Takahashi, "For Silicon Valley Entrepreneurs, Failure Is an Option," *VB News*, October 27, 2009, http://venturebeat.com/2009/10/27/for -silicon-valley-entrepreneurs-failure-is-an-option/.

7. Jenna McGregor, "How Failure Breeds Success," Businessweek.com, July 2, 2006, http://www.businessweek.com/stories/2006-07-02/how-failure-breeds -success.

8. Meg Carter, "Happiness Means Creativity: One Company's Bet on Positive Psychology," *Fast Company*, http://www.fastcocreate.com/1683288/happiness -means-creativity-one-companys-bet-on-positive-psychology.

9. Anita Bruzzese, "DreamWorks Is Believer in Every Employee's Creativity," *USA Today*, July 22, 2012, http://www.usatoday.com/money/jobcenter /workplace/bruzzese/story/2012-07-22/dreamworks-values-innovation-in -all-workers/56376470/1.

10. Ryan Tate, "LinkedIn Gone Wild: '20 Percent Time' to Tinker Spreads Beyond Google," *Wired*, December 6, 2012, http://www.wired.com /business/2012/12/llinkedin-20-percent-time/.

11. Jason Fried, "Workplace Experiments: A Month to Yourself," 37signals, May 31, 2012, https://37signals.com/svn/posts/3186-workplace-experiments-a -month-to-yourself.

12. Jason Fried, "Why I Gave My Company a Month Off," *Inc.*, August 22, 2012, http://www.inc.com/magazine/201209/jason-fried/why-company-a -month-off.html.

10 MAKE IT EASY TO COLLABORATE

1. IBM Institute for Business Value, "Leading Through Connections: Highlights of the Global Chief Executive Officer Study," 2012, http://public.dhe.ibm .com/common/ssi/ecm/en/gbe03486usen/GBE 03486USEN.PDF.

2. Morten T. Hansen and Herminia Ibarra, "Getting Collaboration Right," *Harvard Business Review*, May 16, 2011, http://blogs.hbr.org/cs/2011/05 /getting_collaboration_right.html.

3. Julie Anixter, "Midnight Lunch: How Thomas Edison Collaborated," Innovation Excellence, February 3, 2013, http://www.innovation excellence.com/blog/2013/02/03/midnight-lunch-how-thomas-edison -collaborated/.

4. Dan Zax, "The Curious Magic of Dropbox's Culture-Building, Product-Inspiring Outdoor Hikes," *Fast Company*, January 9, 2013, http://www .fastcompany.com/3004613/curious-magic-dropboxs-culture-building -product-inspiring-outdoor-hikes.

5. Jason Fried, David Hansson Heinemeier, and Matthew Linderman, *Getting Real: The Smarter, Faster, Easier Way to Build a Successful Web Application* (Chicago: 37signals, 2009), chap. 7.

6. Lee Burbage and Sam Moore Cicotello, "Reinventing the Workplace," TEDxPennQuarter2011,12:55–14:08,https://www.youtube.com/watch?v= unVV9O2M0Dc.

7. "GE's Colab Brings Good Things to the Company," *MIT Sloan Management Review*, November 7, 2012, http://sloanreview.mit.edu/article/ges-colab -brings-good-things-to-the-company/.

8. Eliot Van Buskirk, "How the Netflix Prize Was Won," *Wired*, September 22, 2009, http://www.wired.com/business/2009/09/how-the-netflix-prize-was -won/.

9. Janko Roettgers, "Netflix Experiments with Crowd-Sourced Captioning," Gigaom, July 30, 2012, http://gigaom.com/2012/07/30/netflix-amara -closed-captions-crowdsourcing/.

10. Michael Arrington, "Google Has Acquired YouTube," *TechCrunch*, October 9, 2006, http://techcrunch.com/2006/10/09/google-has-acquired -youtube/.

11. Alex Phillips, "Encyclopaedia Britannica vs Wikipedia: A Battle Already Lost?" *Urban Times*, March 17, 2012, http://urbantimes.co/2012/03 /encyclopaedia-britannica-vs-wikipedia-a-battle-already-lost-infographic/.

12. Gamification Success Stories, February 6, 2013, http://mitchellosak .com/2013/02/06/gamification-success-stories/.

13. Bhavya Sehgal and Pronab Gorai, "Platform Strategy Will Shape Future of OEMs: Flexibility to Drive Growth," EvalueServe, January 2012, http:// sandhill.com/wp-content/files_mf/evalueservewhitepaperplatformstrategy willshapefutureofoems.pdf.

14. Greg Bensinger, "Competing with Amazon on Amazon," *Wall Street Journal*, June 27, 2013, http://online.wsj.com/article/SB10001424052702304441404577482902055882264.html.

11 HARNESS THE TIDAL WAVE OF DIGITAL

1. Robert Safian, "This Is Generation Flux: Meet the Pioneers of the New (and Chaotic) Frontier of Business," *Fast Company*, January 9, 2012, http://www.fastcompany.com/1802732/generation-flux-meet-pioneers-new-and-chaotic-frontier-business.

12 HIRE FOR AGILITY

1. Women Worth Mentioning, "Michele Buck, Hershey," May 25, 2005, http://www.womenworthwatching.com/michele-buck/.
2. Dave Ulrich and Norm Smallwood, "What Is Talent?" RBL White Paper Series, 2011, http://www.ikgundemi.com/uploads/6/7/8/0/6780997/whatistalent.pdf.

13 MOVE PEOPLE AROUND

1. Lydia Dishman, "Secrets of America's Happiest Companies," *Fast Company*, January 10, 2013, http://www.fastcompany.com/3004595/secrets-americas-happiest-companies?partner=newsletter.
2. Cisco, "2012 Cisco CSR Report: Our People," 2012, http://csr.cisco.com/pages/csr-reports.
3. Jeff Bezos, letter on career program at Amazon, July 24, 2012, http://www.amazon.com/gp/help/customer/forums?ie=UTF8&cdForum=Fx2NFGOONPZEXIP&cdThread=TxV34LD0G6O9IV.

14 LOOSEN UP

1. The Blog of Tim Ferriss: Experiments in Lifestyle Design, May 21, 2008, http://www.fourhourworkweek.com/blog/2008/05/21/no-schedules-no-meetings-enter-best-buys-rowe-part-1/.

2. Havas Worldwide Global Talent Study, April 2013.

3. Patricia Reaney, "About One in Five Workers Worldwide Telecommute: Poll," Reuters, January 24, 2012, http://www.reuters.com/article/2012/01/24 /us-telecommuting-idUSTRE80N1IL20120124.

4. Society for Human Resource Management, "Yahoo Phases Out Telecommuting," February, 26, 2013, http://www.shrm.org/hrdisciplines /technology/articles/pages/yahoo-bans-telecommuting.aspx.

5. 37signals, blog, https://37signals.com/svn/posts/3064-stop-whining-and -start-hiring-remote-workers.

6. Editors, "Best Jobs," *Outside Magazine*, August 15, 2011, http://www .outsideonline.com/outdoor-adventure/best-jobs/38-Patagonia.html.

7. Aimee Groth and Ben Popper, "These 16 Company Perks Will Make You Insanely Jealous," *Business Insider*, May 18, 2011, http://www.business insider.com/best-company-perks-2011-5?op=1#ixzz2Msxoi3qi.

8. Joe Robinson, "At the Boston Consulting Group, Put in Too Many Hours and You'll Get Flagged," *Fast Company*, May 1, 2007, http://www.fast company.com/59597/red-zone.

9. Full Contact, "Paid Vacation? That's Not Cool. You Know What's Cool? Paid, PAID Vacation," July 10, 2012, http://www.fullcontact.com/2012/07/10 /paid-paid-vacation/.

10. Nancy Messieh, "12 Tech Companies That Offer Their Employees the Coolest Perks," *Next Web*, April 9, 2012, http://thenextweb.com/insider/2012/04/09 /12-startups-that-offer-their-employees-the-coolest-perks/.

11. Melissa Stanger and Aimee Groth, "23 Companies with Employee Perks That Will Make You Jealous," October 13, 2012, http://www .businessinsider.com/companies-with-awesome-perks-2012-10?op=1# ixzz2MswCNwfP.

12. "Morningstar Benefits Package," Morningstar, April 21, 2013, http:// corporate.morningstar.com/us/asp/subject.aspx?xmlfile=186.xml& page=2&filter=.

15   TREAT YOUR TALENT RIGHT

1. Glassdoor, "Employment Confidence Survey," Q4 2012, http://www .glassdoor.com/press/wp-content/files_mf/1357232849GlassdoorECSQ41 2SupplementDRAFT.pdf.

2. Lydia Dishman, "Secrets of America's Happiest Companies," *Fast Company*, January 10, 2013, http://www.fastcompany.com/3004595/secrets-americas-happiest-companies?partner=newsletter.

3. Rob Markey and Fred Reichheld, "Introducing: The Net Promoter System," Loyalty Insights, December 8, 2011, http://www.bain.com/publications/articles/introducing-the-net-promoter-system-loyalty-insights.aspx.

4. Globoforce, "Talent Management Interview with Colin Coulson-Thomas," April 14, 2013, http://www.globoforce.com/globoforce_colin_coulson_thomas_interview.

5. Melissa Stanger and Aimee Groth, "23 Companies with Employee Perks That Will Make You Jealous," *Business Insider*, October, 12, 2012, http://www.businessinsider.com/companies-with-awesome-perks-2012-10?op=1#ixzz2Msvvaavy.

6. Great Place to Work Institute, "World's Best Multinationals," April 14, 2013, http://www.greatplacetowork.com/best-companies/worlds-best-multinationals/profiles-of-the-winners/1522-15-intel.

7. Christopher Caggianom, "Perks You Can Afford," *Inc.*, November 1, 1997, http://www.inc.com/magazine/19971101/1359.html.

8. Dow Chemical Company, "Why Choose Dow: Recognition and Reward," April 14, 2013, http://www.dowcampuschina.com/html_en/s1_choose2.html.

9. Intuit, A New Chapter, 25 Years Proud, "Thanking," April 14, 2013, http://www.intuit25.com/thanking.html.

10. William J. Rothwell, *Effective Succession Planning*, 4th ed. (New York: William J. Rothwell, 2010), p. 47.

11. "100 Best Companies to Work For," *Fortune*, February 4, 2013, http://money.cnn.com/magazines/fortune/best-companies/2013/snapshots/30.html?iid=bc_fl_list.

12. David Rohde, "The Anti-Walmart," Reuters, March 22, 2012, http://blogs.reuters.com/david-rohde/2012/03/22/the-anti%E2%80%93walmart/.

13. Great Place to Work Institute, "World's Best Multinationals," April 14, 2013, http://www.greatplacetowork.com/best-companies/worlds-best-multinationals/profiles-of-the-winners/1511-2-google.

14. Great Place to Work Institute, "World's Best Multinationals," April 14, 2013, http://www.greatplacetowork.com/best-companies/worlds-best-multinationals/profiles-of-the-winners/1528-8-w-l-gore-associates.

15. David Woods, "Performance Management Focus Shifts from 'High Fliers' to 'Average People,' According to Five-Year Study," *HR*, June 11, 2012, http://www.hrmagazine.co.uk/hro/news/1073507/results-study-shifts -performance-management-focus-high-fliers-average-people.

16. Globoforce, "Talent Management Interview with Colin Coulson-Thomas," April 14, 2013, http://www.globoforce.com/globoforce_colin_coulson _thomas_interview.

16 DEFINE YOUR HIGHER PURPOSE

1. Lydia Dishman, "Secrets of America's Happiest Companies," *Fast Company*, January 10, 2013, http://www.fastcompany.com/3004595/secrets-americas -happiest-companies?partner=newsletter.

2. "Mark Zuckerberg Lays Out Facebook's Vision and Strategy," http://vator .tv/news/2012-10-23-mark-zuckerberg-lays-out-facebooks-vision-and -strategy#8rLVGziUA6dWplMt.99.

3. "Mission Statement," *The Economist*, June 2, 2009, http://www.economist .com/node/13766375.

4. Apple, "Jobs at Apple," http://www.apple.com/jobs/us/index.html (accessed April 15, 2013).

5. Tempkin Group, "Employee Engagement Benchmark Study 2013," January 2013, http://www.temkingroup.com/research-reports/employee -engagement-benchmark-study-2013/.

6. Frank Marafiote, "More Than a Paycheck—Offering Employees a Vision," November 19, 2009, http://ezinearticles.com/?More-Than-a-Paycheck— Offering-Employees-a-Vision&id=3282030 (accessed April 15, 2013).

7. Society for Human Resource Management, "Advancing Sustainability: HR's Role," April 11, 2011, http://www.shrm.org/research/surveyfindings /articles/documents/11-0066_advsustainhr_fnl_full.pdf.

8. Rutgers University/Net Impact, "Net Impact's Talent Report: What Workers Want in 2012," May 2012, http://www.heldrich.rutgers.edu/sites/default /files/content/Net_Impact_Talent_Report.pdf.

9. Anne Tergesen, "Doing Good to Do Well: Corporate Employees Help and Scope Out Opportunities in Developing Countries," *Wall Street Journal*, January 9, 2012, http://online.wsj.com/article_email

/SB10001424052970204331304577143212573242048-lMyQjAxMTAy
MDAwOTEwNDkyWj.html?mod=wsj_share_email html.

10. Ibid.

11. Indra K. Nooyi, Speech at Boston College Chief Executives' Club, May 13, 2011, http://www.pepsico.com/assets/speeches/IndraNooyiBostonCollege.pdf.

17 A TALENT UTOPIA

1. "100 Best Companies to Work For," *Fortune*, http://money.cnn.com/magazines/fortune/best-companies/. Companies included in the talent fund index: American Express, Autodesk, Inc., Camden Property Trust, Chesapeake Energy, Cisco, Darden Restaurants Inc., Devon Energy, DreamWorks Animation, EOG Resources, Inc., FactSet Research Systems Inc., Google, Intel Corporation, Intuit, Marriott International, Inc., Men's Wearhouse, National Instruments, NetApp, Novo Nordisk Inc, NuStar Energy L.P., Qualcomm, Rackspace Hosting, salesforce.com, Stryker, Ultimate Software, and Whole Foods Market.

2. Rackspace Hosting did not begin trading until August 8, 2008.

ACKNOWLEDGMENTS

WHEN I THOUGHT ABOUT WRITING A BOOK ABOUT talent, culture, and how great companies act today, it seemed daunting. So much so that we started and stopped this project because it felt too ambitious. What kick-started it again was my belief that it had to be written. For people to hear what we learned. For my company—and for me. Because talent management matters, and how we treat people matters.

As with any endeavor of this nature and ambition, it could not have been done without a team. A huge thank you to our team captain and my partner in crime, Ann O'Reilly. I could fill a book about the amazing contributions Ann has made steering the team and to Havas. She is truly selfless and has done an amazing job driving both the book and me. I would also like to thank Barksdale Maynard. Barksdale led many of the interviews and the research, and he helped to craft much of what we posit. And I also thank Stuart Harris, who drove a great deal of our thinking and who challenged many of our early hypotheses and helped us to push them further.

I would also like to thank the many senior executives cited throughout the book who so generously took the time to offer their insights in interviews with my team and me. This book benefits tremendously from their experiences and expertise and could not have been produced without their help: Mike Abbott (Kleiner Perkins Caufield & Byers), Carlos Abrams-Rivera (Mondelēz International), Randy Altschuler (CloudBlue), Josh Averill (Bank of America), Mike Bailen (Zappos), Chris Benko (Merck), Mark Bergsrud, David Binkley (Whirlpool), Frank Biondi (WaterView Advisors), Deborah Borg (Dow), Peter Bregman (Bregman Partners), Paul Brown, Michele Buck (Hershey), Youngsuk Chi (Elsevier), John Ciancutti (Facebook), Dan Clifford (AnswerLab), Cindi Cooper (Gap International), John Costello (Dunkin'), Jim Crawford (TRIAD), Robert X. Cringely, Bill Damaschke (DreamWorks), Jim Davey (Timberland), Karen Drexler (CellScape), Felicia Fields (Ford Motor Company), Anessa Fike (The Motley Fool), Steve Forbes (Forbes Media), Walt Freese, Dan Gill (Huddler), Chester Gillis (Georgetown University), Rosemary Haefner (CareerBuilder), Kathryn Hall (Hall Capital Partners), Mellody Hobson (Ariel Investments), Tomer Kagan (Quixey), Joe Kennedy (Pandora Media), David Kenny (The Weather Company), Chris Kuenne (Rosetta), Belinda Lang, Michael Leedy (American Eagle Outfitters), John Lettow (Vorbeck Materials), Leighanne Levensaler (Workday), Dave Lewis (Unilever), Laura Maloney (The Humane Society), Sheila Marcelo (Care.com), Stewart McHie (Catholic University), Justin Menkes (Spencer Stuart), Donna Morris (Adobe Systems), Eric Motley (Aspen Institute), Alexis Nasard (Heineken), Jerry Noonan (Spencer Stuart), Bob O'Leary (Citi), Greg Olsen (GHO Ventures), Sev Onyshkevych (FieldView Solutions), Stephen Oxman (Morgan Stanley), Sabrina Parsons (Palo Alto Software), Claudia Patton (Edelman), Paul Polman (Unilever), Michael K. Powell (National Cable & Telecommunications Association), Al Power (Gates Corporation), Robert Price (CVS/pharmacy), Kelli Richards (All Access Group), Ken Romanzi (Ocean Spray Cranberries), Denise Sablone (Grand Circle Corporation), Henry Sauer (Rackspace), John Sculley, Douglas Speck (Volvo), Marty St. George (JetBlue), John Sullivan (San Francisco State University), Kris Szafranski (The Nerdery), Stephanie Tilenius (Kleiner Perkins Caufield & Byers), Brian Trelstad (Bridges Ventures), Dave Ulrich (University of Michigan/Ross School of Business), Dolf van den Brink (Heineken), Dan Walker (The Human Revolution

Studios), David Wilkie (World 50), Arra G. Yerganian (University of Phoenix), Elizabeth Zea (JUEL Consulting), Michael Zea (Aimia), and Ed Zschau (Princeton University).

I am grateful, too, to all those within my own organization, Havas, who took the time to contribute their thinking and offer help in other ways: Eric Ackley, Patrick Armitage, Yvonne Bond, Patti Clifford, Rachel Conlan, Allison Ciummei, Vin Farrell, Madeline Groman, Matt Howell, Sandra Jackson, Amparo Johnson, Bryan Keller, Jared Kreiner, Daniel Maree, Frances Ortiz, Lynn Power, Rhona Press, Emily Rosen, Jane Schlech, Chuck Seelye, Thomas Shim, Allison Waters, and Holden Weintraub. Most especially I would like to thank Lisa Borden at Arnold for working through our earliest efforts and improving the book with each pass.

I would also like to extend my thanks to Laurie Harting, my editor at Palgrave Macmillan, who has seen me through three books in five years. I appreciate everything she has done to help shepherd these books from initial concept all the way through to store shelves.

Finally, and most importantly, I would like to thank my wife, Kate. Thanks for giving me the time to escape on Sunday mornings to research, write, edit, and focus on the book. Taking on a project like this would not have been possible without your support.

INDEX